MENTAL PATIENTS IN TOWN LIFE

Volume 90, Sage Library of Social Research

Sage Library of Social Research

MENTAL PATIENTS IN TOWN LIFE

GEEL -- EUROPE'S FIRST THERAPEUTIC COMMUNITY

EUGEEN ROOSENS

Foreword by JOHN G. KENNEDY

Preface by HARRY L. SHAPIRO

Volume 90
SAGE LIBRARY OF
SOCIAL RESEARCH

 SAGE PUBLICATIONS   Beverly Hills   London

Copyright © 1979 by Sage Publications, Inc.

For information address:

SAGE PUBLICATIONS, INC.
275 South Beverly Drive
Beverly Hills, California 90212

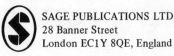

SAGE PUBLICATIONS LTD
28 Banner Street
London EC1Y 8QE, England

Printed in the United States of America

Library of Congress Cataloging in Publication Data

Roosens, Eugeen
  Mental patients in town life.

  (Sage library of social research ; v. 90)
  Translation of Geel, een unicum in de psychiatrie.
  1. Mentally ill--Care and treatment--Belgium--Gheel.
2. Therapeutic community--Belgium--Gheel. 3. Gheel,
Belgium. I. Title.
RC450.B32G48713   362.2'3   79-15386
ISBN 0-8039-1330-3
ISBN 0-8039-1331-1 pbk.

FIRST PRINTING

To my wife

CONTENTS

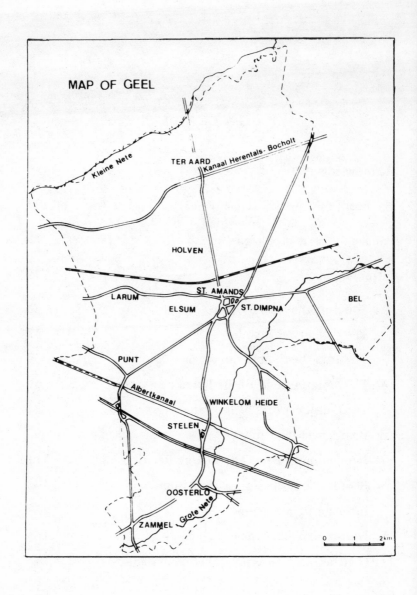

MAP OF GEEL

ACKNOWLEDGMENTS

My thanks go first of all to Leo Srole, Professor at Columbia University and Extraordinary Professor at the Catholic University of Leuven, who designed *The Geel Family Care Research Project* and carried it out with great enthusiasm. His remarkable efforts raised the necessary financial funds for this extensive project.

I owe a great debt to the advisors of the Geel Project: Professor Joseph Nuttin, Ph.D. (Catholic University of Leuven), Chairman of the Geel Project Publication Committee and onetime president of the International Union of Psychological Sciences; Professor Harry Shapiro, Ph.D. (The American Museum of Natural History), who wrote the Preface of this book; Professor Viola Bernard, M.D. (Columbia University); Professor Lawrence Kolb, M.D. (New York State Psychiatric Institute); Professor Jan Blanpain, M.D. (Catholic University of Leuven); Professor Roland Pierloot, M.D. (Catholic University of Leuven).

I must also thank Jan Schrijvers, who greatly aided the anthropological team with his unlimited helpfulness and thorough knowledge of the Geel[1] system, and Leo Lagrou, who introduced me to the Geel Project. His personal involvement maintained the team spirit, for which I am very grateful.

Many Geelians—host families, boarders, and the staff of the State Psychiatric Hospital—have contributed to the writing of this book. Their simplicity, hospitality, and boundless patience have become proverbial to us.

Our work was morally and financially supported by the United States National Institute of Mental Health, the American Family Care Foundation for the Mentally Ill, the Belgian National Fund for Scientific Research, the Belgian Ministry of Public Health, Columbia University, and the Catholic University of Leuven. May this book be a token of our gratitude.

It was a real pleasure working with the other members of the anthropological team. Their considerable contribution to the study will be discussed in more detail in Chapter 3. My special and very sincere thanks, finally, go to Jules Vermeulen, Chaplain of the State Mental Hospital, for his indefatigable and selfless assistance.

NOTE

1. Geel is located 45km southeast of Antwerp.

FOREWORD

In the catalogue of measures which societies have developed to cope with the difficult problems caused by severely mentally disordered individuals, the example of Geel, Belgium stands out. The history of this persistently humanitarian community care system extends back more than eight centuries, which certainly qualifies it as the oldest therapeutic community still in existence. Considering the great amount of confusion which characterizes our modern field of mental health care, it is a cause for wonder that until recently there have never been any attempts to utilize the knowledge which this unique social experiment could provide.

The first significant study of Geel, reported in this book, was carried out by an anthropologist working with a team of other social scientists. They relied on the sensitive techniques of participant observation combined with systematic interviewing, and examination of medical and other records. This comprehensive approach has enabled Dr. Roosens to provide us with a very human account which is yet believably objective. Through it we are led to see how, even though the Geelians have no sophisticated knowledge or even any particular interest in the causes of mental disorder, they have evolved a viable system based on a great deal of tolerance and understanding. Paradoxically perhaps, a basic motivation for the system was self-interest, because the major reason for accepting the mentally ill into people's homes has always been to secure the advantage of their labor and economic support.

How did ordinary villagers institute their humane rules never to call a patient crazy or dumb, and never to stare at a bizarrely behaving individual? How did they evolve their conception that their ties to their own patients are inviolable and immoral to break, and why are they free of fears of psychosis? Where did the norms of responsibility and the townwide alertness to emergencies of breakdown or violence come from? The "boarders" of Geel are most often oligophrenics or chronic schizophrenics who spend a large amount of time in their own idiosyncratic worlds, yet the villagers have developed the working concept that "...a boarder is never totally disturbed. He is always in some way or other socially or mentally normal" (179). It seems clear from this account that all of these rules, implicit and explicit, really evolved very naturally. They did not arise from any peculiar altruism or tradition of Christian love, but from prolonged and daily interaction with the severely disturbed.

As would be expected, however, all is not sweetness and light in Geel, and as in any "ordinary" town, Dr. Roosens has recorded examples of those who exploit the patients, and has shown how the upwardly mobile avoid contact with them. Even the Geelians have been unable to treat the severely disturbed as peers in all spheres of life, as their equalitarian social norms would specify, and they occasionally have to confront the paradox thus created. Subtle discrimination is present, though apparently often below thresholds of awareness, and participation of the disturbed in community organizations is definitely restricted.

Yet even though societal reaction has not been unremittingly positive, the patients of Geel are unanimous in their rejection of the alternative of returning to the mental hospitals from whence they came. They prefer the risks of occasional encounters with relatively benign prejudice, or even ridicule, to which they are occasionally exposed, to any kind of incarceration. That stigma has not been entirely eradicated from the community is unfortunate, though perhaps not unpredictable, yet the reader is not provoked to condemn. Rather, an experience of understanding and empathy is inspired by this account of one of the most interesting and humane systems yet developed, and of the stresses placed on it by modern social change.

There are lessons in the Geel experience for those in the recent movements advocating such solutions as therapeutic communities, half-way houses, board-and-care homes, and other community experiments favoring "normalization" for the mentally disturbed. There is much to be learned by researchers concerned with labeling theory and family therapy, and there is much in this account which can stand as a powerful antidote to the excesses of "antipsychiatry." In addition to its interest to all levels of mental health personnel, *Mental Patients in Town Life* could be read with profit by every concerned citizen.

—John G. Kennedy

PREFACE

The history of the Geel Family Care Research Project of which this book is a part really begins with John Moore and his visit to Geel in 1959. He was at that time vice president of W. R. Grace and Company and later served as the U.S. Ambassador to Ireland. On that trip he was profoundly impressed by what he saw there and, in particular, by the sense of a community concern for the patients who formed so integral a part of the life of the town. On his return to the United States, he came to see me and related his deeply felt experience. I asked him if he would consider publishing an account of his visit and a description of the unique method developed in Geel for caring for the mentally ill. In reply he told me that he had written such an account and hoped to publish it. Soon after that, it appeared in *Look* magazine and the fee that Mr. Moore received for it was contributed to the Family Care Foundation for the Mentally Ill which he had established to support a fellowship program in psychiatry that would enable Belgian physicians to pursue postgraduate studies in the United States.

Shortly after, I was invited by Mr. Moore to become a member of the board of the foundation and as a result my interest in Geel intensified. It was then that it occurred to me that the Geel community richly deserved a special investigation and research study by experts in psychiatry and in the field of care for the mentally ill. I discussed this with Mr. Moore and he responded with enthusiasm. Therefore, I planned to be in Paris in February 1963 and decided to visit Geel to see for myself the conditions there. Mr. Moore made the necessary arrangements for me to meet and discuss with various people in Belgium who might be interested in the project we had in mind. On my way to Geel I had interviews with Jozef L. Custers, the Minister of Public Health, Dr. Rademakers, the retired director of the Geel program for mental patients, and with Professor Piet De Somer at the University of Leuven.

My guide was Dr. Jan Schrijvers who was later to play a very active role in the Geel Research Project.

The initial response to my suggestion for a research program at Geel was most encouraging and I left Leuven in Jan Schrijvers' car headed for Geel with considerable optimism. I was, however, not ready to proceed further until I had actually seen Geel for myself.

I spent the better part of a week at Geel and was kindly and cooperatively taken on a tour to various families boarding mentally ill patients by a member of the supervisory board of psychiatrists. I was, as John Moore had been, strongly affected by what I saw of the system, by the manner of its function, and by the warmth of the relationship between patient and family—an environment that seemed to me so much more beneficial than the isolation and institutionalism I had observed in standard asylums for the mentally ill.

On returning to the United States, the first major advance in organizing the idea of a study of the Geel Program came in 1965 when Viola W. Bernard, M.D. then Clinical Professor of Psychiatry at the College of Physicians and Surgeons, Columbia University, arranged for me to meet Dr. Jan E. Blanpain, Professor of Public Health and Hospital Administration at the University of Leuven. I had, unfortunately, not met him during my trip to Belgium since he was out of the country at the time. With us on this occasion was Dr. Leo Srole, an anthropologist who was Professor of Social Sciences, Department of Psychiatry, College of Physicians and Surgeons, Columbia University. He had recently completed "Mental Health in the Metropolis: the Midtown Manhattan Study," a distinguished and innovative contribution to the study of mental health.

This meeting provided us an opportunity to discuss the prospects of a research study at Geel and to revive the efforts to accomplish it. Dr. Srole expressed an interest in such a study and agreed to assess its feasibility and acceptability to authorities in Brussels, Geel, and the University of Leuven. On his visit to Belgium in January 1966, his task was to win the necessary support and backing of government and academic officials. This he did with great success and agreed to assume responsibility for the planning, development and supervision of the entire enterprise and its funding.

Subsequently, a collaborative Belgian and American advisory committee was established. The Belgian section consisted of Professors Jan E. Blanpain, Jozef Nuttin, Sr., and Roland Pierloot and the American section of Viola Bernard, M.D., Lawrence Kolb, M.D. and Chairman of the Department of Psychiatry, College of Physicians and Surgeons, Columbia University, and myself, Chairman of the Department of Anthropology, American Museum of Natural History.

Field work began in July 1966 and continued until August 1975 with Dr. Jan Schrijvers, trained in the Columbia University Division of Community and Social Psychiatry, as Dr. Srole's assistant and later his codirector. In these positions he was able to contribute significantly to the program. The large number of field workers investigating various aspects of the history of the Geel Program of foster family care for the mentally ill and, in particular, its social, community, and psychiatric aspects were with few exceptions Belgian, most of them associated with the University of Leuven. On the completion of the study in 1975 an international symposium was held at Geel with the presentation of papers by scientists from various countries and the participation of the townspeople with a gala pageant of the legends that account for the origins of this unique development.

This outstanding research program was initially made possible by grants from the Family Care Foundation for the Mentally Ill established by Mr. Moore and the Foundation's Fund for Research in Psychiatry. Later, generous grants were made by the Grace Foundation, the McDonough Foundation, the U.S. National Institute of Mental Health, the Belgian Ministry of Public Health, the University of Leuven, the New York State Psychiatric Institute, and the Columbia University Division of Community and Social Psychiatry.

The results of this decade of research will be covered in an omnibus volume nearing completion, tentatively entitled "Community Remarkable of the Western World: Geel, Belgium 1475-1975." Dr. Leo Srole is its senior author with Dr. Jan Schrijvers its principal coauthor. It represents a synthesis of some forty study units.

The present monograph by Dr. Eugeen E. Roosens, Professor of Anthropology, Catholic University of Leuven, is an integral part of this research program and provides an illuminating analysis of certain phases of the Geel experience. By providing essential insights into certain aspects of the Geel community it is a contribution of importance.

—Harry L. Shapiro

INTRODUCTION

In the last decade, antipsychiatry—represented by such authors as Cooper and Foucault[1]—has seriously challenged the role of the mental institution. These institutions are accused of further degrading so-called deviant persons by submitting them to a bureaucratic, authoritarian regime that isolates them from normal life and thus deprives them of many opportunities for mental improvement.

These and many other charges may be exaggerated, but the question remains whether it is good to bring together people with different types of mental disturbances and handicaps and to compel them to live in an artificial, less normal world. Many people, professionals and others, are concerned about this problem.

A few years before the emergence of antipsychiatry, specialists in social psychiatry at Columbia University in New York, in collaboration with their counterparts at the State Hospital in Geel and the Catholic University of Leuven (Belgium), had wondered whether the Geel family care system did not present a model for an alternative system. Indeed, for centuries ordinary families in Geel have been taking patients into their homes and offering them an opportunity to live in a normal environment. Moreover, the 'boarders' are free to move about in the local community: They may walk unaccompanied through the streets, go to movies and soccer games, and visit bars. Nor are they obliged to live with other patients. Would not Geel offer exceptional opportunities for the improvement of, as well as a human environment for, 'chronic patients'?

Everything started with this question. But at the time there was no clear answer. What was known about Geel in the early sixties was limited to general impressions.

Nobody could give a reliable or accurate account of what was happening with the hundreds of patients (more than 1,300) lodged with families throughout the community. Therefore, a serious research project to determine how far the Geel system offered a suitable alternative to traditional institutions did not seem a redundant luxury.

Second, for purely scientific reasons it seems useful to reconstruct as faithful an image as possible of the Geel system and, on the basis of this model, to ask a series of scientific questions. Indeed, Geel may be considered as a natural experiment, offering an exceptional opportunity to examine what occurs when, generation after generation, hundreds of mental patients are housed in a normal community and are allowed to move about rather freely. Do the ill become healthy, or vice versa, as the popular local saying suggests: 'Half of Geel is all crazy and all of Geel is half crazy!' Does the normal environment have a favorable effect on the patients? Can the patients cope with their freedom? Is it possible for normal Geelians to live with the patients? Is community life fundamentally disturbed by their presence? These are natural questions when many mental institutions regularly need to deal with complaints that their patients 'debase' the neighborhood or make it 'unsafe' just by walking in the streets.

The Geel system allows many such questions to be asked and answered, and this is why the Geel research project developed into an extensive multidisciplinary enterprise.

Considering that the Geel community has been boarding patients at least since the thirteenth century, it would have been unwise not to take the opportunity to trace this system throughout the centuries. Several historians of the Catholic University of Leuven have recently completed this task.

A team of psychiatrists and psychologists have examined whether boarding patients in families has a therapeutic effect. One of them, F. Cuvelier, has already given a positive answer to this question in a fascinating work on the interaction between boarders (patients) and members of host families.[2] Sociologists have studied the development of the Geel situation with respect to the types of families that take in patients, and have examined the problem of whether the family care system can resist growing modernization. An answer to this question is given in R.-M. d'Hertefelt-Bruynooghe's book.[3]

The results of the other related studies are still being worked out.

We, the anthropological team, were asked to study how the patients are dealt with outside the host family within the wider context of the local community. This is an important question because the integration or reintegration of mental patients into a normal environment is now being discussed more than ever. More and more voices are demanding that modern society no longer discard its mentally disturbed members by isolating them; nor, they assert, is it ethical that society thus be kept comfortable and 'hygienic' for the sake of those without such handicaps. Many share this feeling. However, the question remains whether seriously disturbed or mentally retarded people can be realistically offered an opportunity for a life worthy of a human being outside the walls of an institution.

Apparently Geel has succeeded in doing so.

Mental Patients in Town Life: Geel—Europe's First Therapeutic Community attempts to sketch the interaction between Geelians and boarders in various situations of public community life. It is a description and an analysis that tries to remain close to its objects, and in this sense, it is 'objective.' It also avoids value judgments, whether approving or disapproving, as much as possible.

In this book, which is the result of our empirical study, I attempt to present the reality as directly as possible to the reader by such devices as quoting field notes that portray a vivid picture of the Geel situation. Still, this book is more than simply a documentary. While observing, a social scientist asks questions and examines phenomena with questions in mind. This allows the scientist to point out things that may escape the casual visitor or the journalist.

NOTES

1. K. Trimbos, *Antipsychiatrie. Een Overzicht,* Deventer, Van Loghum Slaterus, 1975.
2. See the bibliography.
3. See the bibliography.

The Church of St. Dympna. The exorcisms were performed in the attached building.

Main entry to the State Psychiatric Hospital.

Chapter 1

SITUATING THE GEEL SYSTEM

Geel is known worldwide for its mental health care in a community setting[1], and in the last few years, the Geel system has attracted attention as an alternative to institutional treatment. Although other successful systems do exist where mental patients function in one way or another in everyday life, the Geel care system has been in existence for centuries and the patient population in the community is rather high. Today more than 1,300 patients live among the 30,000 inhabitants of Geel, and at certain times in the past the number of patients has risen to more than 3,000. This makes Geel unique.

But Geel is also interesting from a purely behavioral viewpoint. When taken as a natural experiment, the Geel system enables us to see what happens when more than 1,300 mental patients are allowed to live among a normal population. It is not surprising that the recent *Handbook of Social and Cul-*

tural Anthropology considers the description and analysis of the Geel system as one of the most urgent tasks for psychological anthropology.[2]

In former years, Geel differed more from 'medical institutions' than it does at present. Many institutions where mental disturbances are treated have evolved considerably in recent years. The social and psychological dimensions of what have been called 'mental illnesses' are recognized, and teams, in which psychologists and sociologists work with physicians and psychiatrists, attempt to see the patients as much as possible as total human beings and treat them accordingly. Gymnasiums are being built for patients and the usefulness of play and work therapy is being recognized. Patients have more social life than before, for example, they can go to coffee shops. But one thing cannot be avoided: their company is primarily composed of people suffering from some form of mental handicap or disturbance. No matter how earnest the attempt to normalize their environment, institutions remain institutions, and from this point of view, Geel is different.

This does not mean that Geel has an ideal or perfect system. Several objections have been raised against the Geel method. Some say the Geel system may provide a solution for 'hopeless' cases, but that it is less adequate for people who have a chance for recovery or for significant improvement. Patients may improve slightly and stabilize at Geel— they will not recover. For this type of patient, they say, it is better to be admitted to an institution where more intensive care and professional attention can be provided. Such a view is perhaps not without foundation, but there always are some mental patients who prove to be incurable even when given the best possible care.

Moreover, not all institutions have the means to provide adequate patient guidance. This will be so for many years to come, especially in poorer countries. So the establishment of some variant of the Geel system as an alternative to expensive institutional care is still worth consideration. And it is not necessary to adopt all of the present Geel system. Family care of a certain type of patient can be combined with the establishment of a therapeutic unit providing more intensive and professional care. In Geel itself such adaptation is being considered.

The history of Geel patient care has been described in detail by the members of the *Geels Geschiedkundig Genootschap* (Geel Historical Society), as well as by the team of historians collaborating with the Geel Project. Readers interested in this history are referred to these reports, some of which have already been published.[3] Here, we will restrict ourselves to an outline in order to situate and introduce our own study. We shall borrow extensively from an unpublished paper by K. Veraghtert.

The Geel system has undergone important changes during the course of time. In Geel everything began with belief in miracles and supernatural intervention; today one is confronted with a secular state institution almost completely outside the influence of the Catholic church and religious faith.

Historians agree that the Geel care system originated from the cult of Saint Dympna that was celebrated in Geel. It has been shown that as early as 1250,[4] mentally ill people were brought to Geel to seek cures from St. Dympna. According to the legend (or should we say myth?) St. Dympna was the daughter of an Irish king who, after the death of his beautiful wife, fell in love with his own daughter and attempted to marry her. Together with St. Gerebernus, her confessor, the girl supposedly fled to Flanders in order to escape her father's incestuous passion. She was traced by her father and caught in the Geel region. After her confessor had been put to death, she let herself be decapitated by her father with his sword rather than submit to his dishonorable and repulsive demands.

Structuralist anthropologists may find food for thought in this story. All the elements are present for an intricate analysis: an attempt at incest; a father who kills his own daughter, and that by means of his sword; an asexual confessor, and so on. Local exegesis, or ethnoanalysis interpreted the matter more simply: St. Dympna became the patron of the mentally ill and their cure because, by her heroic death, she defeated the evil spirit that had entered into her father to drive him into a rage and madness. As madness was attributed to possession by some evil spirit, the cult of St. Dympna becomes clear.

The popular interpretations of the origin of the cult of St. Dympna are not uniform. In 1863, P.D. Kuyl wrote: "From long ago, St. Dympna has been venerated as a patron of the senseless, particularly because she heroically defeated her father's frantic and mad love."[5] A.C. Van Der Cruysen has another interpretation: "On the highest peak of the arch stands forth the solemn image of St. Dympna on a small pedestal, treading on two crushed figures, representing the vices to which most of the causes of mental illness are attributed: Haughtiness and Impurity."[6] Whatever the interpretation of the Dympna cult, for centuries the cure that patients sought in Geel was involved with religious cult, ritual, and symbols.

This ritual, which was celebrated from the first centuries of family care until 1797 when the church was closed by the French revolutionary armies, was performed at the Church of St. Dympna. The therapy consisted mainly of a religious rite. The patients were allowed into the church and later into the special 'patients' room in groups of nine, and for nine days exorcisms were administered. In these centuries, the Geel therapy was surprisingly simular to the rites found in other preindustrial cultures: symbols and rituals wielded by initiates in a socially recognized framework formed the core of the therapy.[7]

Due to the growing influx of patients in Geel, the Church authorities appealed to the inhabitants of the village to house the pilgrims. Some patients, or their families, expressed the wish that the pilgrims remain in Geel. Thus, the boarding system originated: the patients were taken into host families and remained there. According to historical reconstructions, a common denominator ran through the entire history of the system[8], a principle that is still unchanged: the economic dimension of the system seems to play a decisive role in the orientation of patient care in Geel. Since the 17th century the increase in the patient population in Geel correlates directly with financial considerations. From that time onward the welfare agencies of the Flemish area sent their poor patients to Geel because it was less expensive to lodge them in the village than to confine them in an institution. It is difficult to determine the importance of the religious factor, but one thing is certain: The determining force of Geel has ceased to be solely religious, or magico-religious, if this ever was the case. Up to the end of the 18th century, however, the entire system remained under the supervision of the local chapter of canons, and the rites and the care of the boarders were the responsibility of the Catholic church.

As we have already mentioned, the Church of St. Dympna was closed in 1797 after the French revolution. Although pilgrimages could no longer officially be held, the family care system was continued. Here, too, the economic factor was decisive. In order to reduce costs the city of Brussels closed down its own mental institution in 1803 and sent more than 100 patients to Geel. Many other cities and their welfare agencies did the same, so that the number of boarders in Geel gradually increased from 200 around 1800 to 400 in 1820 and to over 900 in 1850.

The living conditions of the patients at that time cannot be compared with those of today. All kinds of patients were sent to Geel, including the 'bad' and aggressive, at a time when modern sedatives were nonexistent. Some had to be put in irons, some were chained to the wall, and some had to be physically overpowered. The majority of host families were poor farmers and the boarders shared their living conditions. A report written in 1841 dealing with the situation in the Belgian institutions, however, showed that the patients were no worse off in Geel than anywhere else.

In 1850, the Parliament passed a law intended to improve the living conditions of mental patients. The *Kolonie,* as the Geel hospital was called, was placed under the supervision of the minister of justice, and in 1851 a special regulation was issued determining the modalities of the administrative and medical care. The principles underlying this regulation are still operative. Since the midnineteenth century, patient care in Geel has been primarily the concern of the Belgian State. The role of the ecclesiastical authorities was restricted to a minimum, and although the nomination of the chaplain was already provided for in 1851, it was implemented only in 1892. The role of religious rites receded into the background and continued to decrease until the 1960s when even the folkloristic St. Dympna procession was abolished. Under the influence of renovating trends in the Church, the parish priests felt that these things should be recognized for what they are: legends.

Many host families, to whom we spoke about the cult of St. Dympna, thought the abolishment of the procession a sad thing. Not that they believed in the healing power of the saint, but because it was a loss to Geel. Many older or middle-aged persons from host families remember when they went on pilgrimage to St. Dympna with their parents and their patients. All now admit that they themselves have given up that practice. Only one patient, who lives in the parish of St. Dympna and goes to mass daily, remarked that St. Dympna helped her in her life. The pastor of St. Dympna Church, who is in charge of the Dympna cult, said he almost never sees pilgrims any more, but that, remarkably, he receives many letters from various parts of the world and particularly from the United States. These letters ask for prayers or masses, and monetary offerings are usually included. Some are people who feel assailed by some form of mental illness and, in a desperate and tragic way, seek help in often impossible circumstances.

It is obvious that the 'medicalization' of the entire domain of mental illness (an historical process against which many objections are presently being raised) together with an overall tendency toward secularization are responsible for the decline in devotion to St. Dympna. By the intervention of the Belgian State in 1850 and the appointment of nonecclesiastical personnel, it has been accepted in Geel that mental disturbances are primarily the concern of 'doctors,' and not of 'pastors.' Meanwhile, under the influence of science, a consensus has developed within the Catholic church about the nature of mental illness. No longer is it considered to be caused by diabolic possession or to be the consequence of an impure or licentious life. Miraculous healings are not mentioned in present-day Geel, and only with difficulty could we trace one case of a sudden recovery that the patient attributed to the intervention of St. Dympna.

Today the Geel family care system is almost entirely separate from the Church.

One historian of the Geel Project, Karel Veraghtert, on whom we have heavily relied for writing this chapter, attributes the rapid increase in the number of patients up to the late 1940s to the constant and significant improvement of the patients' situation. Administrative and medical services were organized, and since 1862 the patients could obtain special treatment in the infirmary of the Kolonie. The requirements demanded of the host families concerning meals and lodging for the patients became much stricter. About 1900 there were close to 2,000 patients in the town, this figure increased to 3,736 in 1938. This peak has never been exceeded, and in 1944 the number of patients had decreased to 2,600. Today there are still about 1,600 patients[8]. There are several reasons for this decline, but the financial factor has played a crucial role. The medical staff of the Kolonie is underpaid, and thus it is difficult to attract candidates for vacant positions. This obviously reduces the capacity of the medical services. Nor are the benefits paid to the host families very attractive, so that here too the care level remains well below what could be attained. All this does not help the institution's reputation in professional circles. Since the social security system developed in Belgium, people from less well-to-do classes are also able to appeal to institutions other than welfare agencies. Many prefer this solution.

The *official* name of the former *Rijkskolonie* was changed a few years ago to "Rijkspsychiatrisch Ziekenhuis—Centrum voor Gezinsverpleging" (State Psychiatric Hospital—Center for Family Care[9]). The 'State Psychiatric Hospital' is located in a rather old-fashioned appearing complex of buildings and performs various functions in the Geel system. The candidate boarders are admitted to the 'hospital' for observation; the sick and the boarders who have become 'recalcitrant' are brought there; and elderly patients who can no longer be placed live out the last period of their lives there. In this sense, the 'hospital' is an integral part of the Geel system. It also serves as the regional psychiatric hospital.

The Center for Family Care, for its part, concerns itself specifically with the boarders and the host families and also provides the outpatient service of the hospital. In practice it is difficult to separate the hospital from the center. The hospital is completely independent of the center only in its role as regional hospital: Admitted patients do not necessarily go into family care even if they are found suitable.

Between the hospital and the center (or the host families) there is a continual reciprocal flow of patients. For the years from 1966 to 1976, the average number of patients admitted from the families to the hospital per month was:

1966	1967	1968	1969	1970	1971	1972	1973	1974	1975	1976
83	80	86	84	91	89	83	88	77	75	82

This comes to an average of 2.7 patients *per day*.

From the hospital an average of one to two patients *more*

go to the families than are admitted per week. Per day this averages out to 2.7 to three patients leaving the hospital.[10]

Admission to the State Psychiatric Hospital at Geel occurs as in any other Belgian hospital. Dr. H. Matheussen, the present director of the institution, described the admission procedure to family care as follows:[11]

"Admission of a new patient is, obviously, subject to selection criteria. The referral authorities present a patient through psychomedical, social, and psychological reports. These are discussed by our psychiatrists and, in practice, a number of pragmatic criteria are applied that have evolved from experience and that match the desires of the host families and their development."

"There are, first, the *fixed* requirements. The language of the patient is of primary importance since it is the first and foremost instrument of human communication. Thus, the patient must be Dutch-speaking. Then there is the criterion of mental functioning: the elementary necessity of self-care and maturity in crisis situations in the family. The IQ can serve as a rough guideline for this: it must be at least 70-75. Age also has to be taken into consideration: sufficient physical capacity is necessary. Finally, there are counterindications: syndromes with pronounced personality disturbances (psychopathology, toxicomania) and paranoid psychoses. We have also come to the opinion that, in the current context, a committed patient—both broadly and strictly speaking—is no longer to be considered, as a matter of principle."

"There are also the *optional* criteria. Put negatively, the syndrome may not show pronounced mood variations in the sense of short cycles with a large range. Positively, not only definitely chronic patients can be placed in a family, also patients with subevolutive pathology can be assigned."

In contrast with earlier centuries, the patients are now selected in a specific manner. It is important to keep this in mind in order to understand properly the interactions between the Geelians and the patients that are analyzed further on. Extreme 'uncontrollable' patients are not placed in the families. Experience seems to have demonstrated that, for these people, life is not possible in an open, normal environment.

After preselection the patient is admitted for observation. The patient is invited one or more times to the weekly meeting of the medical, social, and nursing staff. If the candidate seems suitable for family placement, the candidate is brought to the family by a district nurse.

Of the one-third 'psychotics' and two-thirds 'oligophrenics' (the terminology of the Rijkskolonie), two-thirds of the total boarder population are men and one-third are women. In 1975, 5.8% of the population of Belgian mental institutions were in Geel; in 1945 this figure was 11.4%.

Geel is divided into 10 nursing districts. For each district there is a nurse who works under the direction of a supervisory nurse and a psychiatrist. The patient is visited regularly by the district nurse, about once every two weeks.

In recent years, the center has taken various initiatives for the benefit of the boarders. Work therapy and individual creative activities within the context of the boarding families are now possible under the supervision of a teacher. There are sport clubs and a fishing club for the patients. As we shall see further on, the center organizes regular outings and trips for the patients, even to Spain and the French Riviera.

The host families and their boarders thus have available a rather extensive infrastructure which they can fall back on. Although the Kolonie is generally not looked on with favor by the Geel public, it does, with its various services, contribute significantly to the creation of a sphere of safety for a large number of Geelians. If a patient should get out of hand, one knows where to turn, and help is always there.

Although the number of patients has decreased to about 1,600 and even less, it is still remarkable that so many mentally retarded people live together with 'normal' people in one town and that most are lodged with families.

As we have mentioned, F. Cuvelier has shown in a recent study that the interaction between the host family members and the patients is such that it leads to an enrichment of the patient's possibilities of expression, and thus has a therapeutic effect[12]. The patients are given a place and a role in a process of mutual acceptance. From 'wanderers' they become people who have found a home.

This work is limited to the study of the patterns of interaction as they develop between boarders and Geelians *outside the context of the host family* in the wider surroundings of the local community.

NOTES

1. See K. Veraghtert, Geel: Nationaal en Internationaal Verplegingsoord. In *Geel. Van Gisteren tot Morgen,* Geel, Lions Mol-Geel, 1976, pp. 492-507. Also H. Eynikel, *De Uitbreiding en de Beoordeling van de Gezinsverpleging van Geestes-zieken. Uitstraling van het Schotse en Geelse systeem (1850-1970),* Leuven, Faculty of Philosophy and Letters (M.A.thesis), 1971; M.P. Dumont and C.K. Aldrick, Family Care after a Thousand Years. A Crisis in the Tradition of St. Dympna. *American Journal of Psychiatry,* 119 (1962) 2, pp. 116-121. See also R.-M. D'Hertefelt-Bruynooghe, *Gezinsverplegingspatronen te Geel. Een Socio-logisch Onderzoek vanuit Kostgezinnen en Patiënten,* Leuven, Universitaire Pers Leuven, 1975, pp. 15-28.

Geel is not the only place in the world where family care previously existed or existed for a lengthy period of time. On Iwakura, Japan, see C. Greenland, Family Care of Mental Patients. *American Journal of Psychiatry,* 119 (1963) 10, p. 1,000. On nursing localities in France during the Middle Ages, see P. Gominet, *Contribution à l'étude de l'assistance des malades mentaux en place-ment familial,* Paris, Faculté de Médecine, 1962, pp. 13-14. See also H. Eynikel, op. cit.; R.-M. D'Hertefelt-Bruynooghe, op. cit., pp. 16-19; H. Binswanger, Die Familienpflege im Kanton Zürich 1901-1936. Medizinische Erfahrungen. *Monatschrift für Psychiatrie und Neurologie,* Beiheft 87 (1939), pp. 1-128. On the family care system in Lierneux, Belgium, see J. Chantraine, Evolution actuelle du placement familial psychiatrique des adultes à Lierneux. *Acta Neurologica et Psychiatrica Belgica,* 68 (1968) 6, pp. 392-406. On the attitude toward Geel, see G. Hedebouw, *Houding ten aanzien van Geel en de Geelse Gezinsverpleging. Overzicht van Onderzoeks-resultaten van het Sociaal-Psychologisch Team van het Geel Family Care Research Project,* Leuven, unpublished report, 1975.

2. See J. Kennedy, Cultural Psychiatry. In the work mentioned, edited by J. J. Honigmann, Chicago, Rand McNally, 1973, p. 1183.

3. See K. Veraghtert, unpublished paper read at the 'Internationaal Symposium over Gezinsverpleging voor Geesteszieken' (International Symposium on Family Care for the Mentally Ill), Geel, 15 and 16 May 1975.

Idem, De Overheid en de Geelse Gezinsverpleging (1660-1860). *Annalen van de Belgische Vereniging voor Hospitaalgeschiedenis*, 1969, VII, pp. 113-127; Idem, De Krankzinnigenverpleging te Geel (1795-1860). *Jaarboek van de Vrijheid en Het Land van Geel*, 12, 1973; M. H. Koyen en M. De Bont, *Geel Doorheen de Eeuwen Heen*, Geel, 1975; H. Eynikel, Geel, Bakermat van de Gezinsverpleging. *Annalen van de Belgische Vereniging voor Hospitaalgeschiedenis*. 9, 1971, pp. 113-123.

4. This is an hypothesis of the historian, Mr. Bellemans (oral communication). Other scholars consider documentation from the fifteenth century to be the first *absolute* proof of the existence of the boarding system. But these documents allow one to suppose that the system had already been in operation for a long time.

5. P.D. Kuyl, *Geel Vermaerd door den Eerdienst van de H. Dimphna*, p. 77.

6. See also M. De Bont, De H. Dimpna. In *Geel*, pp. 467-476.

7. See M. De Bont, ibidem, p. 471.

8. K. Veraghtert, unpublished paper, 'Internationaal Symposium'.

8. At the time we carried out our study (1969-1974), there were 1,361 patients lodging with 1,007 host families. The others stayed at the hospital. At this time host families were allowed to board a maximum of two patients. Very recently some families have been allowed to take in a third patient. All the patients boarding with one family must be of the same sex.

9. There are approximately 300 people employed by the combined institution.

10. See J. Segers, *Sociologische Doorlichting van het R.P.Z.-C.V.G.*, unpublished report, 1977, p. 13.

11. See 'Nationale Studiedag over Gezinsverpleging', unpublished text, 1975, pp. 2-4.

12. F. Cuvelier, *De Interaktie tussen Psychiatrische Patiënt en Geels Pleeggezin*, Leuven, Faculty of Psychology and Pedagogical Sciences (thesis), 1974. Idem, Een Gastgezin als Kleine Therapeutische Gemeenschap. *Tijdschrift voor Psychotherapie*, 1 (1975) 2, pp. 71-79. Idem, La famille nourricière de Geel comme micro-communauté thérapeutique. *L'Information psychiatrique*, Vol. 52, no. 8, October 1976, pp. 915-930.

Chapter 2

THE PATIENTS OR BOARDERS

In order to make the very general terms of 'boarder,' 'schizo-phrenic,' and 'oligophrenic' more concrete, we shall describe 11 patients as they are seen by their host families or by other Geelians. These descriptions will be briefly supplemented by what we ourselves were told by the boarders if they spoke to us.

We would like to stress that we have consciously avoided all psychological, depth psychological, and analytic terminology. In the course of the study it became clear that there is nothing to be gained by classifying the patients into clear-cut categories, however learned these categories might appear to be. Only one distinction is obvious to us: that which is made between people who, in one period of their life, were normal or relatively normal and only later began to behave in a deviant manner, and those who never have fully developed mentally. The Geelians also distinguish between the cases that clearly fall into one of these two categories.

But even from this perspective, there are still borderline cases and those who come 'in-between.'

The people of Geel themselves do not place any scientific labels on the boarders—there are no 'paranoids,' no 'manic depressives' in Geel. But there is a distinction made between 'good ones' and 'bad ones,' which we shall discuss at length in Chapter 10. What is striking is that the boarders are considered primarily as individual persons, with their own peculiar tics and often with their own worlds. As we were often told, "Every boarder is different." The anthropological approach that we apply here maintains this 'emic' perspective.

Patient 1

The deviant behavior of this patient is considered typical of someone who constantly 'flips' or 'misses the mark.' His host parents are elderly people. P himself was well known in Geel and many people were familiar with the stories about him. People used to call him 'God' or 'The King.' We met him when he was 80.

The patient received us in front of the house where he was sweeping the sidewalk. P immediately started to talk.

He was given another 600 years, he said, because he was God himself. His mother is the Blessed Virgin. Our Lady does not look at all like the apparition in Puurs (a Belgian village). She is dressed all in white, as you can see her in the living room or in the church, but not as people represent her. She is a normal human being. Every night she tells P what to do and not to do in order to go in heaven. There are lots of bad people. The Blessed Virgin still has many relatives on earth.

This is the second time he came to earth. This time until 1933 (sic). He has suffered a lot. He has two mothers. P has also visited hell. The devil is about three feet tall. He is not black but the color of smoked herring. He cannot harm P but comes and tries to see what he can do.

P's 'earthly' mother had 11 children. His father was an alcoholic. P himself has two daughters and one son. One of his daughters visits him two or three times a year (this was confirmed by the host family). What could they do with him at home? If they knew who he was, they would not treat him like that! But that must remain a secret. P still goes for short walks. In the past he used to walk as far as Bel and Mol (neighboring villages).

The pastor bases his wisdom on the Bible. The pastor and the pope depend on the authority of P. P reads the newspaper because of the accidents. P is against things that are not allowed. Naked women are filthy. One must be decent and honest. Television is a matter of money. P likes people. He has come back to earth to clean up the planet once more. People do not go to church anymore like they used to. He cannot intervene anymore with the liberals, socialists, or Flemish nationalists, because his identity card is not valid (as a patient he has lost his civil rights). He is God and King but not of this world.

Heaven is high up there. The moon is only the halfway point. One enters heaven through a trapdoor which is no bigger than the top of a table and which opens and closes. It is very spacious up there. In hell it is terrible. From up there you can see it all. Hell is under the Scheldt River (P was raised in Antwerp). The damned cry and shout. One of them has slept with his own daughter. Socialists are there, too. Where does God, his Father, come from? He is the Son. God the Father never married. Gabriel appeared to P's mother. She gave birth to him. And they say she was a whore! Everything will be settled after another big war. That war will start at 2 p.m. and end at midnight. That war is pretty close already, only one or two years away.

Every night P walks through 18 streets and when the bells of St. Andrews (Antwerp) toll at 11, the Blessed Virgin appears on the clouds. As soon as she has called him she disappears. He talks to her in heaven and the next morning he writes down what she has told him. (We have seen two big plastic bags filled with the patient's notebooks. With his permission we were allowed to read some of them.)

P went to school in Puurs. He was poor. He was there with
schoolmaster N. He was very good at mathematics and pen-
manship. His mother could not afford it any longer. His
father worked on the docks and always came home without
money. He drank a lot. His mother went around with a
pushcart to sell sand. She got 'water in the legs.' 'She was a
good woman.' P went around with sand when he was only
11, accompanied by his two sisters. They started at seven in
the morning and went around until five or six in the evening.
After having been with a farmer for some time, from whom
he did not get any money at all, he went to Antwerp. His life
with his wife was unfortunate. She was married to him but
slept with her father as well. His father-in-law had pushed P
to marry this daughter, but he had made a hole in the
bedroom wall so that he could come and sleep with his
daughter (P's wife).

His children should go to church. To them he can still give
happiness. He will not send them to hell. In heaven there is
singing and lots of fun. There, people do not eat nor drink.
There are palaces which cannot be found anywhere else.

NOTE: P's host family confirmed that he repeats these
        themes over and over again. His notebooks contain
        the same sort of thing.

Patient 2

This patient only 'flips' from time to time and is said to be
a 'good one.' She has a reference system which at many
points coincides with that of her social environment. She
works well, is a good cook and 'a good woman.' Usually her
behavior deviates only with regard to religion and eroticism.

Both her host parents are 70, and have always had patients
in their family. Presently, the family is composed of the host
parents, the wife's brother, an unmarried son, and two female
patients. P2 is 86 and has been living with the family for 50

years. The other patient is a middle-aged woman who has
lived with the family for four years.

According to the father, young people do not accept
patients any more. They asked for another boarder when
they remodeled their home seven years ago. With the money
they received for the patient they intended to pay for the
remodeling.

Though P2 is 86, she still works around the house. She
cooks very well. She has always worked well and has no fits.
But she always tells strange stories, which she frequently
repeats. Once it happened that she was at the hospital of the
Rijkskolonie when a child was born. She claims they are the
chaplain's children and are given a fertilizer ('magnesia') so
that they grow up fast. When she was young she dated men.
She wrote letters to her neighbors proposing marriage. People
knew about it but did not react. Now she does not talk about
it anymore. She is very religious. She goes to mass every
Sunday, prays before meals, is a member of the Association
of the Sacred Heart, and says the rosary. Every year on the
day after Pentecost Sunday, her family comes and visits her.
"She is a good woman." Everybody gets along well with her.
She talks a lot to herself, and so does the other patient. They
do not talk to each other much. The other one is very
short-tempered. One day she pulled the host mother's hair in
a rage. P2 immediately came to her aid. The other patient
does not go to church. She constantly moved during the
Mass. But she does do some errands.

P2 wants to be young. Recently she dyed her hair with
shoe polish. She has many fantasies. She does not really tell
lies. She said the doctor had examined her and found that she
was pregnant. She also tells (and repeated this in our presence) that she always wanted to be a priest, but she was
refused. She is very fond of priests. Other men are too risky.
Priests are not. The others take you to bars, and the like. She
claims she was engaged to a boy who later became a priest.
Her mother-in-law is a child of St. Dympna. She also loves

Saint Joseph as well as the Blessed Virgin who gave birth to a divine son. She says that people become very tiny again when they are old, as tiny as a little ball. She is afraid of that.

P2 does not eat meat on Fridays. She would like one more ember day. What is everything coming to?

Patient 3

This patient suffers from epilepsy and regularly has 'fits.' Her 'deviant behavior' is not overtly based on marked delusions. For the host family she is primarily someone who is difficult to live with. Her fits of epilepsy, however, clearly mark her as an ill person.

The host father always had boarders in his family, but the mother moved to Geel from another town. The patient used to live with the host father's mother. She arrived in 1957 as a 16 year old.

On certain days the patient readily speaks to the host father. She frequently dates men. She goes out dancing, but does not tell her host family. She likes to watch 'hot' movies on TV. The host mother then turns the TV off or switches to another channel. P did not approve of the host father's marriage, but now she causes less trouble about it and leaves him alone.

An epileptic, she has about two fits per month. When she is on her period she is also quite troublesome and throws tantrums. The host family ignores her. They do not react. The host mother, however, must do her utmost to restrain herself. P makes a lot of noise and slams doors. The family acts if they do not notice. They cannot always cope with her.

P is very good with children. She is considered a child herself. The children always share things with her. P still plays a lot of children's tricks. P is French-speaking. She is practically incapable of writing. She tries to read, however. She likes going to get the mail and reading it herself. P fears that she will have to leave. P sometimes goes on vacation with an uncle of hers. Her parents are both dead.

P is not miserly. She does not go to the movie theater because it is too far away and there is a TV at home. She collects family pictures, postcards, and funeral cards. P says that when she was a little girl someone tried to kill her. She claims it was one of her uncles. She had a Flemish mother. Her family is somewhat peculiar. According to the host father, 'something is wrong there.' In recent years, her uncles have come several times. They would like to try to find a job for her to exploit her. P has a sister in the Kolonie. They see each other sometimes, but they cannot put up with each other too well. They do not see each other often.

P receives medication to control her epilepsy. The host family tries to keep the children away when she has one of her fits.

P lies a lot. She invents things to clear herself. She must be watched as she is inclined to steal money. She does not run errands and she is never given money. P does not like to be with people. She does not attend church services, except, perhaps at Christmas. In church she is calm, but she stares at everyone and thinks that everyone stares at her. P is very unsociable when there are visitors, but she will often eavesdrop on conversations. She also listens through the door of the host parents' bedroom. She is jealous of the wife and expresses this directly and overtly. When the light in their bedroom stays on for a while, she will react the next morning. She never wants to go to bed before the couple. The wife is annoyed by this. P regularly sticks out her tongue to the wall.

P pleads for the children. She sometimes spoils them a little. Her best friend used to be the four-year-old boy. They have given him another place at the table so as to separate him from her.

The host family will not take any other patients, primarily because of the children. They are relieved when P goes on vacation, but they do not want to get rid of her now that she is there. P likes it there very much.

The host father's family tried to insinuate things about him. They would have liked to have had P so she could work for them. They had told H that P had to stay with the cows when they had to calve. They also said that she had to work too hard. P refused to change places.

P wants to know everything down to the last detail. When she goes to the baths (of the Rijkskolonie), she has a friend. P takes very good care of the host family's handicapped child. Her sister tries to get money from her.

Patient 4

This patient almost never 'flips,' but is domineering, 'dogged,' and rebellious; she is a particularly aggressive person. The endoculture defines her deviations, not as those of some-one who is 'flipping,' but rather as manifestations of bull-headedness, obstructionism, constant protest, and bossiness. Altogether, this is not normal.

Both host parents have always had patients in their fami-lies. They had their last patient taken back by the Rijksko-lonie a few months ago. Now she has been placed in another family. The host family itself has had four patients who have gone home cured. They were not cured by means of medica-tion. The host family thinks that boarding is disappearing because young people no longer want all the trouble, and they do not need this source of income.

The patient that was sent back to the Kolonie gave them a lot of trouble. She had many fits and beat and grabbed the host mother. The husband was ill for a time and had to stay in bed. P then also stayed in bed and did not want to get up. The district nurse had to intervene. P was very fat. She weighed about 230 pounds. She did not actually steal, but she sometimes took small things. She also sat in the sunshine to get a tan. When she was on her period, she was very untidy. She did not want to work. P made passes at men, so she had to be watched constantly. She was not raised Catho-

lic and neither prayed nor attended church services. She
could not converse. She always sat next to the stove. She did
not speak much. When she had to do something she made a
lot of noise. P's relatives have never been seen. She had been
with the host family for three years.

Sometimes P tried to dominate. She banged the table. She
felt that the host father, of whom she was afraid, was
growing weaker due to his illness, which caused her to feel
more in control. P practically never went out. She remembered a lot. "You wouldn't say she was a patient." Her face
was always washed, but from sheer stubbornness she dirtied
her pants. She could have helped herself very much. Twice a
day she dirtied her pants and put them in the closet. The wife
was not allowed to enter the room and had to wait until the
patient had gone to the baths in the Kolonie (every two
weeks) to clean up P's room. P was given drugs to calm her,
but they did not help.

The host family has had many 'good' patients who were a
great help. All patients are different.

Patient 5

This patient is a 'good patient.' He is only slightly retarded
and is incapable of working on his own, according to the host
mother's diagnosis. The vast majority of patients in Geel are
not of this type.

P has been living with this family since 1942. The host
father died in 1969. Both host parents have always had
patients in their families. The wife's family has housed 'bad'
patients, who carried knives. The many children of the family
are all married. The mother thinks that there are still people
who want to house patients for the extra money. "The
people of Mol, Balen, etc. are envious of those of Geel for
their having laid aside a little money."

P is of Walloon origin, but speaks fluent Flemish. He
speaks very well and sometimes accompanies Dr. Y of the

Rijkskolonie. He helps a little with everything. He never 'misses the mark,' although he is a little retarded and sometimes a bit childish. He has a beautiful handwriting. He does not steal. "He lies a lot, but he is company for us." P does not lie to deceive, but rather to attract attention. He used to chase girls, but that has improved. He is very hot-tempered, but that has improved also. He never breaks anything nor is he sloppy or dirty. He attends Sunday mass unaccompanied, and fulfills his Easter duty. He was probably a Catholic before he came to Geel. He still talks about his village and sometimes about the parish priest who was his godfather. He regularly goes to soccer games and to the *Klimop* of the Kolonie.

The host family has never met any of P's relatives. P was very neglected when he arrived in Geel and claims to have lived in a trailer. He is incapable of doing work by himself. He says to others that he is *not* ill. He is able to read and write and enjoys writing and receiving letters. He is happy when he can communicate with others. He has some friends in the Kolonie and goes with them to soccer games. Dr. Y of the Rijkskolonie calls him a 'colleague.' P went to the Rijkskolonie to work when his host family stopped farming. P is good with children. He collects things like stamps and cards. He is clever. He does not dream much, though sometimes he says: "My left ear has been whistling again." The host family always agrees with him. P sleeps well. He washes himself. He often goes for walks, but returns soon. He does errands, always very well, and always gives back the change. P smokes many cigarettes and sometimes cigars. He likes to watch children's programs. Sometimes he switches to the French-speaking channel. P switches the TV set on and off himself. When the program does not please him, he turns it off. He likes detective and cowboy films. He is also in charge of the fishing and soccer clubs at the Rijkskolonie. P used to carry a lantern in the St. Dympna procession.

Patient 6

This patient is a 'bad one,' who is likely to stay that way. The host father said that the patient talks too much—he never stops. Always the same confused things again and again. The host father regularly asks him to be quiet. If the patient reacts strongly against this, however, he lets him go on. P comes from a very old and very rich Belgian family. He is shabbily dressed but it is obvious that he has fine manners. He speaks Dutch and French. The patient has finished secondary school and is now 40 years old. P does some simple errands during the week, e.g., getting the milk and buttermilk for the family. He knows which days he must do this. He doesn't go to mass. For that matter, the pastor advised against it. Sometimes P watches TV, but he does not like soccer. The host father thinks that P does not sleep much. P speaks continuously about the Germans (the World War), about executions in Dachau. He does not care for women and only once did he say: "I would like to marry N. (the daughter of the host family)."

P spontaneously began to speak as we sat there. According to normal standards, his story is not coherent.

"I was the first in Rhetoric (the last year in secondary school in Belgium). I still believe firmly in the Blessed Mother. I was the tennis champion in school. My mother sent me to a Catholic school. Impurity. Most of the children said 'murderer' to Christ. Severe teachers. I had to undress in front of my governess. Since then, I am losing all the parts of my body: my hands, my teeth, half of my head. War is not so bad. The bread of the Lord. I don't know if he exists. At school they taught me that I must be a Catholic. God kills people. He must allow time to restore the world. Original fruit. When you die, there will be many. . . . The devil made death. The evil vice. There are many crazy people in Geel. I am afraid of death. The devil puts that in my head. Death is stronger than life. Murderers let God disappear in his greatness. I don't want to die before I have saved the world. In the Bible, God is the most holy. The world is good now and has always been good, but the satans have always tried to murder God. I am very afraid of the murderers. I can't go to Brussels. Hell is the devil, and the devil takes men, more and more. He first takes a drop of blood. My hand is from God. Hands are evil. I am called to become a priest. I'll let the young people go free and scold them. I am a JOC-ist (Jeunesse Ouvrière Catholique: Young Catholic Workers) and a JOC-ist must be silent! I get my hands back when one does a miracle. I am possessed by an impure spirit; it is completely naked. My niece is a lost case, my nephew also runs around naked. Grandmother hit me in the belly unjustly but she has relations in the gendarmerie. I am impure and I think that such a person cannot do much with a pastor. I commit mass murder nights in my pot. Nights. The end of the world is coming: death first. *Sin is everywhere! Maurice is my friend because one must love one's enemy. I saw God very young.* (The italicized sentences were said in French.) When you sin you have to go to confession."

According to the host father, the patient repeats the same themes over and over if one does not make him be quiet. The host father thinks that you cannot talk with him. "It's been many years since anything has been said to him."

Patient 7 (From a report by Dr. R. Bouwen, who lived in
              Geel for many years.[1])

This patient is faithful, misjudged, and in Geel terms 'a very good one.'

"From the day we first came to live in Geel, patients came regularly and often to our house. We lived on a farm that was close to the center of town so we could sell a great deal of dairy products and vegetables at home. Such routine errands were mostly done by patients so we had daily visits from a fixed group of customers."

"J came every day very early in the morning with her jug to get milk. Before anyone else in the house was up, she would rinse out her jug and bravely set out. In the summertime, it was a pleasant walk for her in the early morning sun, but in the winter and the rain, too, she found her way through the darkness and the cold. Shivering from the cold and with numb hands—she either wore gloves that were worn out or she had lost them—she would come into the warm cow barn and watch the animals being taken care of. Every day she had a lot of news to tell and things to talk about that she had gathered from her many errands or that she had learned from acquaintances that she had met on the street in the early morning. Everybody knew J and both the policeman on the beat and the early morning mailman were sources of information for her. Accidents, family dramas, plans for the future, changes, visits of one or the other—all these things gave her subjects for extended conversation. She could talk for at least an hour each day without becoming boring. After J had left every one of us was fully informed about everything there was to know about what happened since the day before. After her talk in the barn she would normally come in to the living room for awhile to say good morning. A few jokes would be made and she would give her commentary without becoming annoying. J would be in a very good mood and would then go home."

"She was about 55 years old at the time and was a small woman. Her left hand was slightly crippled. She had broken two fingers once and, because of poor care, part of her hand remained stiff. She was very lively and was particularly good at conversation. She was what they call in Geel 'a very good patient.' After awhile she told me that she had never known her father and had only kept a few pictures of her mother. She had been raised by her aunt and when the aunt died, she was brought to Geel. At the time, she had been living 20 years with the same host family. The father of this family was a teacher and there were six children. It could be said that the children were taken care of by her for years, if not raised by her. She did all the housekeeping, helped with the cooking, and when 'Madame,' as she had to call the host mother, was away took care of the children.[2] After awhile J became truly indispensable to the family. She herself was contented with the work she was given to do."

"After she had been coming to our house for years, J began to talk more and more about her host family and less about the news of the day or of the happenings in the community. The children had grown in the meantime and far from being able or allowed to take care of them J became, according to her, the butt of their ridicule and dissatisfaction. Mainly though, her complaints centered on the conduct of 'our Madame,' as she called the host mother. It mostly concerned objectively small things and the events that make up concrete family living. She was no longer allowed to answer the door or to brush off the suits of 'Mijnheer.' She was also given special dishes and silverware to use. Once one of the children rinsed off his plate before beginning to eat because J had done the dishes but not well enough to suit him. On this occasion, she had to hear herself be called a sloppy woman, and so on."

"From then on, each morning she came to our house and talked about these things and complained particularly to my father who let her talk while he did the chores. She told my parents all the intimate things of the host family, their difficulties with each other, with the children, between the husband and wife, and so on. This often took place while we all sat together at the breakfast table. She insisted particularly that we not say anything about this to 'Madame' or 'Mijnheer.' My father once suggested that she ask the doctor from the Kolonie to change something or to put her with another family. But for her this was by far the greater evil. She had gotten older (about 65) and was sometimes sick or not feeling well. She wanted this hid for as long as possible out of fear that she would be taken to the Kolonie. She suffered the most from what she called the 'ingratitude' of her host family. 'When the children were small, I was needed to wash and feed them and to put them to sleep. Now that they have all grown up, they are looking for a way to get rid of me without having people talk.' "

"In the family where J lived, the mother gave birth to the sixth child in her later years, without she herself or the members of the family being aware that she was even pregnant until a few hours before the birth. Such a 'wondrous' birth naturally causes a great stir in a family, and J, of course, told us everything about it down to the smallest detail. Among other things, she told us the following: 'Some of the people in the stores in Geel had already asked me, "Well, J, is your madame pregnant again?" I answered that she hadn't told me anything yet but that it could well be true. I didn't dare say anything about it against 'our Madame,' although I really thought it could be so. She would certainly get mad if I dared to interfere. I also knew that she actually didn't want any more children.' "

"J has now gotten old. Long walks tire her, her shopping bag has begun to get heavy, her sight is failing, and she is often unwell. She still lives with the same family but she now lives her own life somewhat apart from the affairs of the family. Last year I only met her a few times. She knows she is getting old and sees, with pain in her heart, the day approaching when, because of her health, she will be taken to the Kolonie."

Patient 8

A patient who is well integrated into 'public life,' 'someone who can take part in everything.'[3]

"E also came every day with his jug to get milk or to buy eggs. He is now about 35 years old, tall, and has a youthful appearance. He walks with long, rolling steps. One could call him a very sociable type of errand boy. He presents himself very politely and somewhat shyly, but is nonetheless very punctual and scrupulous with his errands. His manner of speaking is childlike, and he feels very friendly to the children around him. When he would come to our home, he would be immediately interested in the children's games. He could join in enthusiastically when hide-and-seek was being played, but he gave the impression of having a strong sense of responsibility when, for example, the play became too rough, when a fight threatened to break out, when it was time to go home or to do his errands. E wanted to be taken 'seriously' and he would talk about 'grown-up things' but with the frankness and spontaneity of a child for whom everything that is good is good and all the rest is bad. The farmworkers would sometimes tease him by getting him worked up by contradicting him about one or another sport hero. E would sometimes be led on quite a ways, but when he realized he was being teased, he could react very angrily and would 'write off' the individual concerned. People for him were either good or bad and he would say it frankly."

"He lives in the family of a district nurse from the Kolonie together with another boarder who is middle-aged. His position is somewhat that of an older child in the family. His most important job is to take the children to school and to pick them up again. He also does the errands. So he is often on the streets and everyone knows him. Whenever something is happening, E is there and he talks about it to the people he meets. Recently, E noticed on his way home from the school that the traffic lights weren't working at the crossing on Passtraat. He figured they had to be fixed as soon as possible. He also knew the most effective way to go about having it done. He went immediately to the chief of police. E said, 'I thought that I should go right away and tell my friend, J. I went to look for J at the police station and we went together right away in the police car and J said, "Tell me, E, where does that have to be fixed." We opened the switch box together and everything was fixed.' E goes to the High Mass at 10 o'clock every Sunday at St. Amands Church. He is a friend of one of the singers, who lives next door to him, and he also knows the sacristan very well. So he can always sit in the choir loft. He is always one of the first ones there. He arranges the chairs for the singers, puts the music books in order, and distributes them when the singers come in. He finds out from the sacristan which mass will be sung and he tries to show each one the right pages. He knows that there must be silence in the choir loft and seriously admonishes the singers who sometimes ignore this rule. The sacristan is generally the first to start making comments on what is happening in the service and during the sermon, and even he doesn't escape E's strong reprimands. It becomes a kind of game between the sacristan and E—making comments and being reprimanded—until E gets annoyed. The singer, whom E knows very well, then intervenes and makes a quick end of it."

"In the host family where E stays, there is a rivalry between him and R, the second boarder. They vie with each other to get the favor of the lady of the house by doing all kinds of household chores. She told me that this sometimes degenerated into scuffling. One word from 'the master of the house' is sufficient to settle things."

"During his free time, E generally stands on the sidewalk in front of his house. He can sometimes stand there dreaming and not see the passers-by. Generally, however, he is all eyes and ears for what is happening in the street: he greets the people who go by, exchanges a few words, speaks with the neighbors and with the customers of a seed and fuel dealer who lives across the street. It could be said that E is truly one of the patients who help form the image of 'Geel and its patients' in the street and in public life."

Patient 9

This patient was cured, and stayed.[4]

"Every evening, R also came to our home with a pail to get milk for his host family and for other people in the neighborhood. He was about 25 years old, rather small, and had a boyish appearance. He usually would stay talking a long time about the things that neighbors talk about. He could speak about housekeeping, animal care, adversities, and illnesses in the family almost as well as an intelligent housewife. In this respect, he demonstrated a deep sense of responsibility. He lives with a farmer's family where the children were married but still came home regularly to help their father in the barn and in the fields because he was already 70 years old. R lived with these people since childhood. It was difficult for him to walk then. He was subject to regular epileptic attacks but for the rest was normal as far as his intellect and character were concerned. As he grew older, these epileptic attacks completely disappeared, but R continued to live with his host family as he had never known any other. He did vacation regularly with people in Tongerlo (a neighboring community) with whom R had stayed for a few years when this family still lived in Geel and who still considered him a member of their family."

"Now R lives alone with the mother who has been a widow for a few years. Before her husband died, he was sick and bedridden for a long time. In this period, the wife was also often confined to bed and then it was R, with the occasional help of one of the children, who did the housework from the cooking to the washing of the linen and also tended the two cows that the people still had. When the husband became critically ill, R took turns with the other children in sitting up with him. He called the doctor or the priest when it was necessary. R also addressed his host parents as 'Father' and 'Mother' as the children did."

"Now R is the great support for the old lady and he realizes it fully. In spite of her poor health, she can still stay in her own home and have her own household."

Patient 10

This patient was a 'bad one' who changed gradually into 'an excellent fellow.'

The patient is 36 years old. He went to school until he was 14 and afterwards went to work in a bakery. However, he soon ended up in an orphanage. From there he came to Geel. He has been 20 years in the same place and lives with three unmarried brothers, middle-aged men, who work a rather large farm together. P's father, a miner, has visited him only once. P recognized him, but ran away. He didn't want to see his father. P's mother is dead. Once one brother came to visit. According to the host, "It's in the family." All of P's brothers have been committed to psychiatric institutions. His father was a drunkard and would beat his mother. The children got nothing to eat at home.

According to one of the hosts, P was 'a bad one' for a long time. They tolerated it. Now it is much better. Now and then he still gets his 'whims.' He worked himself up recently until he was raging mad "because his bed was too narrow." He kept it up until he got a new bed. P does not take any medication and nothing is prescribed for him. P cannot stand men in the house and only when he is alone does he feel he is in control.

P always used to work with the mother of the three unmarried brothers until she died. So P is capable of doing all the household chores. On Saturday P does the shopping for the whole week. Everyday he cooks for 'the family,' does the dishes, makes the beds, and cleans the house. In short, he has taken over all the housekeeping. P is mad when the leaves fall, and then he sweeps around the house all day long. He also gets mad when it rains because then the house gets dirty.

P is very communicative. He says he has only one complaint: when it rains and thunders his knee hurts from an old strain. "I is here for 20 years already!" He feels completely at home. P stresses that he "does everything here." He does not want to leave. He would only like them to take his name off the register of the sick (to declare him cured), then he would be completely satisfied. "You're not in Geel for nothing!" Mother was a very good person. "I don't have a girl friend and I wouldn't want to get married. That doesn't interest me.

When I see a woman ride by on a bicycle who is well built, I would really like it if I could catch her! I am well off here, what more do you want?" P dreams a lot about women. He also watches them on TV. He goes to the movies on Sundays but does not go dancing. He likes children's programs on TV a lot and prefers sports and movies.

Patient 11

About a patient who was no longer considered suitable to stay with a host family, the host mother told the following:

"They came to get Whitey (a nickname). They said that he had assaulted a girl. This isn't true because he even went to take girls home (as a trusted chaperon). He threatened people. And that was probably true, because he would often do it as a joke. He would act as though he had a knife in his hand. He took one of the girls home to a country house (there are many small summer cabins around Geel). But that was too much! Because precisely at that moment there was another woman with the fellow who lived in that cabin, and Whitey saw that! (So he was accused of something he didn't do.) Other people saw it too—responsible people of about 70 years old. In fact, these people came to me afterwards and proposed tearing down the cabin, but I told them they shouldn't do it because someone would certainly find out. Otherwise they could have done it! Adultery is really something nowadays."

"Whitey was beaten up and given shots to make him confess. They didn't let him smoke either. In X (a psychiatric institution) he suffered still more. Then he went back to his family, but after three months they sent him back because in the city they can't stand such people! He really was a joker. He used to disguise himself and blacken his face and if anyone was scared, he said: 'You don't have to be afraid, I'm only Crazy Whitey!' Only one time did he hit someone, N. He was the leader of the bunch that broke the windows of the Z bar. This guy had buried Whitey's radio."

"Whitey collected garbage, delivered coal, delivered gas bottles, collected football pool tickets, and also helped the farmers. He was very trustworthy—even in money matters. He also had a lot of money. I still have about 9,000 francs (about $225) for him. He did drink quite a bit, but not always beer. He also drank coffee all day long. He was with us for 31 years from when he was 16 years old."

NOTES

1. R. BOUWEN, *Sociaal-Psychologische Studiegroep (Rapport Geel-Projekt)*, 4, pp. 17-18.
2. Normally, the patients address their host parents with the very familiar *Moe* (mu) and *Va* (fa).
3. Ibidem, 4, pp. 19-20.
4. Ibidem, 4, pp. 21-22.

Chapter 3

TOWARD A JUSTIFIABLE APPROACH

We originally planned to report on the Geel community. It may be questioned, however, whether Geel is indeed a community in the technical sense of the word. From the perspective of patient care, we are dealing with a well-defined area: Patients of the Rijkskolonie can only be boarded out within the administrative boundaries of Geel. But this alone does not make Geel a 'community,' and many things indicate otherwise.

Insofar as something like a 'community' exists in Geel, i.e., a social entity that is typologically clearly distinguishable from other analogous constituencies, one would expect most people to know each other. In present-day Geel, with its 30,000 inhabitants spread over a territory of more than 25,000 acres, this is impossible. Geel is not a small country village; in area, it is one of the largest towns in Belgium[1].

Geel may best be described as a conglomerate of different localities whose nuclei correspond to the 12 parishes. Nearly all of these parishes have, until recently, been more or less small villages. But today four of these nuclei have geographically merged, and all others, with the exception of the village of Bel, are interlinked in such a way that there is no sharp territorial or sociological distinction between them. Although Geel has a center and a periphery, it is impossible to indicate precisely the borderline between the rural and the more urban parts.

It was further impossible to reconstruct the 'social structure' and the functioning of the Geel system for each of the 12 parishes. This time-consuming activity would have required years of field work and in many respects would not be relevant to the researcher primarily interested in studying the social relationships that have developed between the 'normal' Geelians and the patients of the Rijkskolonie outside the context of the boarding families.

The complicated debate over 'community studies' (asking whether the 'community' has any consistency as an object for sociological or anthropological research because indisputable definitions have not yet been established) has shown at least one thing: The 'community' or whatever it is called, can be studied as a network of relationships that have, at least in part, a local basis. Because the patients of the Rijkskolonie may not leave the Geel territory without permission and then only on special occasions, it is certainly appropriate in this case to conduct a network analysis of the relationships between the 'normal' Geelians and the patients of the Rijkskolonie.

Concerning these relationships, we asked four primary questions:

(1) With whom do the patients, outside the boarding family, have social contact?
(2) What is the general nature of this contact?
(3) What can these contacts tell us about the social identity of the patients in the social network of Geel?

(4) How is mental illness and retardation perceived by normal Geelians and what sociopsychological techniques do they apply in living with them?

To answer these questions, we combined different research techniques.

We interviewed the heads of all the host families (about 1,000) concerning the nature and frequency of the social contacts that their patient(s) had with outsiders. We formulated the questions as neutrally as possible and simply asked with whom and how often within a certain time-span the patients made outside contacts, how often they go for walks, and the like. In asking these questions, we deliberately refrained from 'qualitative matters,' such as describing the interaction between the patient and nonmembers of the family. The reasons for this were several. First of all, we considered such 'qualitative' information as basically unreliable due to the bias which some of the host families might have: Answers might be given in the context of what is considered ideal for the patient. For example, a person might say that the patient is treated as 'a child of the family' by the relatives of the host family, that they see to it that the patient goes only to 'decent' bars, and the like. Moreover, it might be assumed that a certain number of host families could not describe the nature of the relationships between the patient and outsiders in a precise manner.

By using an instrument consisting of short, neutral questions we tried to avoid such complications. Doubtless, our success is not complete, but because we have interviewed the total population, it may be assumed that the errors will not be enormous, even if systematic distortions are possible. To this, two other guarantees can be added. Jules Vermeulen, Chaplain of the Rijkskolonie, the interviewer, was himself a born Geelian who knew the system from the inside, having grown up in a family that always had patients. All the host families knew this. They also knew that the chaplain is privy to 'inside information' about the patients, so that 'stories' would not be readily accepted. A second guarantee was that the answers to the questionnaire's main inquiries were verified with other techniques applied independently by other researchers. For example, the number of patients in the movie theater has been counted twice. From participant observation in bars, estimates could be made of how many patients visit bars, independently of the answers given on the questionnaire. Some questions were asked twice, so the answers could be checked against one another.

In order to gain a better insight into the content of the relationships, members of the team became participant observers in the community.

R. Bouwen, a psychologist who lived in Geel for part of his youth and adult life, and E. Roosens, an anthropologist (the author of this book), concentrated on the interaction patterns between patients and Geelians in the streets and at festivities and other public events, such as church services.

W. Van Eyen, a psychologist and anthropologist, noted as accurately as possible, and with special attention to the language and expressions used, what happened between patients and other Geelians during 106 visits to 43 of the 143 bars of Geel.

Using the anthropological procedure of nonrepresentative sampling[2], E. Roosens conducted approximately 110 interviews with host families and prominent personalities of Geel who are very familiar with the system. These interviews were formally open, although they were indirectly oriented to the patients' social relationships. Most of these interviews were extensive, lasting on an average for one and one-half hours, and dealt with the subject as thoroughly as possible.

In addition to the 1,000 interviews concerning the patients' social network, Chaplain Vermeulen also conducted 1,000 other interviews concerning the patients' religious practices and the way in which the host families apply traditional ethics to the patients' behavior. With these interviews we tried to determine how the Catholic church, through the host families, influences the patients' behavior. The same researcher also interviewed the committee members of all the 87 Catholic voluntary associations of Geel. Participant observation was unnecessary here as no patients were interacting members of the associations.

J. Cools, a sociologist, conducted 130 extensive interviews in all the families of Bel and carried out participant observation in this locality for six months. He, too, is a born Geelian. He recorded as many reported events and anecdotes from the past as possible, and also studied the genealogies of the inhabitants of Bel. The results of the Bel study are not included in this book and will be published later. We did, however, take them into consideration when preparing this study.

We approached the village of Bel from as broad a spectrum of fields as possible, in the style of traditional ethnography. From the literature concerning methods in ethnography, it has long been clear that an ethnographer can never include all the dimensions that could theoretically be studied[3]. Although we were well aware of this limitation, we still tried to include as many aspects of the sociocultural system as possible, as well as to trace their histories. In our plan, the Bel study constituted a case study in which we tried to examine the relationship of the factors we studied in the overall context of Geel to the other sociocultural dimensions. At the same time, the Bel study was intended to provide a diachronic dimension to the network of the patients' social relationships.

Strictly speaking, Bel is not representative of the whole of Geel. But it is a part of Geel, and in this way an accurate picture can be obtained about what happens between the ill and the healthy 'somewhere in Geel,' in a setting described as faithfully and in as much detail as possible.

In addition to the more descriptive-analytical problem (as presented in the Bel Study), an anthropological-theoretical problem is studied as well. The hypothesis that often changes in the infrastructure affect everything else is once again confirmed. One hundred fifty years ago, the residents of Bel did not take in patients. Bel was primarily inhabited by relatively wealthy farmers who looked down with some contempt upon the 'crofters' of Geel who needed patients to make their farms profitable. When farming in Bel deteriorated, partly because the large farms refused to use chemicals thus diminishing the crop yield per acre as compared to what it was elsewhere, their profits decreased and they had to call in cheap labor from the hospital. From then on, patients were also employed there. Bel, in the eyes of downtown Geelians, has now become a 'remote' part of Geel and, as there are only three farmers left with profitable farms, nearly the entire population is dependent on factory work elsewhere. The number of patients has decreased, and there is a remarkable correlation between the housing type and the presence of patients. In only one of the 36 modern houses built in Bel does a patient board. All other boarders are lodged in older, farm-type houses. In other words, Bel may be considered as a kind of exhibition ground where a population made up almost exclusively of farmers has changed into one made up mostly of industrial workers, and where the process, which is taking place in all of Geel (where there are still over 230 farmers), has occurred faster and more visibly in a 'mechanical' way.

The above questions unavoidably lead to the problem of the patients' social identity insofar as it can be reconstructed on the basis of social relationships outside the family. They also raise the question of the status given in Geel to mental illness or handicaps. Is the boundary between the healthy and the sick disappearing in Geel?

We shall try to answer all of these questions from a specific point of view: that of social anthropology. Our approach is neither psychological nor psychoanalytical. This means that we have looked primarily for crystallized average behavior and norms in the Geel system of caring for patients. Wherever possible we have used statistical techniques, but when this was impracticable, for theoretical or practical reasons, we used other methods. Areas that seemed to be important have not been ignored simply because they could not be approached in a quantitative manner.

We shall examine the structural and functional nature of the network of social relationships in Geel. Nothing will be said of the *psychological* meaning of the system for the patients. Our study will give an approximate image of the interaction between Geelians and boarders outside the context of the host family. We shall observe that the system runs quite smoothly if it is considered as an instrument to enable mentally handicapped persons to live outside a hospital. We shall also examine in detail what opportunities for interaction are offered the patients and to what extent they make use of them. What is denied the patients will also be investigated.

Before we attempt to give a quantitative survey of the different types of social context in which the patients participate in Chapter 5, we shall first sketch the general, moral, and human atmosphere in which the boarding system operates. We want to emphasize that the figures reported in the quantitative survey are fluid, i.e., they reflect the situation at one particular moment and since have changed.

NOTES

1. A. Pals-Ghoos, Structuur van de Gemeente Geel. In *Geel,* pp. 315-329; Idem, Demografie. In *Geel,* pp. 345-364.

2. On 'nonprobability sampling' see J. J. Honigmann, Sampling in Ethnographic Field Work. In R. Naroll and R. Cohen (Eds.), *A Handbook of Method in Cultural Anthropology,* New York, Columbia University Press, 1973, pp. 267-274.

3. See B. and J. Whiting, Methods for Observing and Recording Behavior. In R. Naroll and R. Cohen, op. cit., pp. 282-286.

The main street of Bel on a weekday morning.

Traditional farming methods.

Chapter 4

THE MORAL ASPECTS OF THE BOARDING SYSTEM

Several publications on Geel present the family care system as a product of Christian brotherly love. Geel is claimed to be a symbol of the love for the least fortunate of humanity—the mentally ill[1]. The same image of Geel is found in brochures and pious writing intended for the mass of the faithful or for tourists. Geel is called 'The Charitable Town.'

Even though this approving epithet contains a germ of truth, it seems totally misleading to so characterize present-day family care. The attribution of this quality to Geel undoubtedly is linked with the religious origin of the town as a place of pilgrimage for mental patients. As has been described in the introduction, patient care emerged from pilgrimage practices dating back as far as the thirteenth century, and probably even earlier. While the pilgrims who came to St. Dympna to invoke a cure for their mental illness waited for their turn to be let into the 'sick room,' they were boarded with the townspeople. This created the family boarding system. Considered in this historical context, Geel can well be called a 'charitable town.' Up to the late nineteenth century, the so-called treatment of the mentally ill was more like ill-treatment. In many countries patients were confined in prisonlike institutions. In Geel on the contrary, they lived with families, were free to walk around in the village, and were to a certain extent allowed to participate in community life. Compared to what was happening elsewhere, it was indeed not inappropriate to consider Geel a shining example of brotherly love and humanitarianism and to call it a 'charitable town.'

We often came across this expression during interviews with host families and leading personalities from the Geel region. But, as our investigation progressed, it gradually became clear that this label gives a very inadequate image of what inspires present-day family care. We became convinced that there are not many Geelians who, at the start of their patient boarding career, took in a patient out of sheer brotherly love.

In some exceptional cases, brotherly love may have been a component of this motivation, but generally things were otherwise.

The Geel family care system as it functions today has, in the eyes of the people themselves, nothing to do with charity, heroism, or Christian love. None of the 40 priests living in the Geel community has a patient from the Rijkskolonie. From interviews with about 20 of them, it was clear that no priest sought the slightest excuse for this state of affairs. No one seemed embarassed, although patient care was explicitly discussed. The reasons for this became gradually clear: In Geel patient care is not viewed as an act of charity bestowing a halo of moral greatness on the host family. Several Geelians involved in the project as researchers and all the pastors of Geel declared positively that patient care is never discussed as if it were an act of charity—not during Sunday services, nor at meetings of Christian associations or societies. This is not a matter of tactfulness with respect to the patients, for no patients attend those meetings.

One of our colleagues, Jules Vermeulen, himself a priest and chaplain of the Rijkskolonie, asked, at a meeting of Geel priests why the patients of the Rijkskolonie were never mentioned as one of the 'minority groups' so often talked about in sermons and speeches. The reaction was general amazement. No one had ever thought of this. A few were slightly ashamed, but all admitted that they had never viewed the patients in this perspective.

An investigation among the executive committees of the more than 80 Catholic organizations in Geel showed that this question resulted in the same reactions as with the priests[2]. Many organizations had collected money to aid developing countries or the handicapped at home and abroad, but nobody had ever associated the Rijkskolonie patients with one of these categories. One specific case is particularly revealing. An association was established in Geel whose main object was to promote the integration of handicapped persons of the town into the existing organizations. The association also concerned itself with the integration of the mentally ill people from the local community. Yet no one had ever had the idea of involving the Rijkskolonie patients. The thought had simply never occurred to anyone, our interviewer being the first to bring it up.

All these facts indicate that, in the present sociocultural context, boarding is not directly linked with Christian love or sensitive morality. To almost all Geelians who are involved with family care or have been so at one time or another, boarding is a morally neutral concept. One simply takes in a patient or not. And if one does so, one can always take the matter to heart, or neglect the patient, or treat the patient well or badly. A host family may be good, bad or in-between, just like a teacher, pastor, or carpenter.

During the more than 2,400 interviews with host families and other inhabitants of Geel, on the occasion of countless other contacts over a period of three to four years, and in the course of six months of participant observation, the members of the team only once encountered a spontaneous mention of brotherly love as the chief motive. This was with an aged couple whose seven children were married. The woman said she had taken in a patient out of Christian love and explicitly stated that she considered family care a Christian duty. She did not need the money, nor the help of the patient, who, in this case, was economically inactive. Her husband, who was present at the interview, remained rather aloof from this statement.

Concerning patients, expressions such as 'they're only poor fellows' or 'losers,' 'sick people are human, too,' and the like, are often heard, but these statements refer to patients who are already present and not to the motivation for taking a patient into the home in the first place.

If the motivation to take in a patient is not primarily, or even at all, a matter of altruism, humanity, or Christian love, then what is it?

We will approach this problem indirectly. In our opinion, it would be an unreliable procedure simply to ask the host families themselves what their motivation was, and end motivation research there. Although comment on this question of motivation was extracted during some 80 interviews with host families and community leaders from Geel (and the answers were practically uniform), we thought it best also to analyze Geel speech and crystallized cultural features concerning this subject, as well as to utilize relevant sociological observations.

Key words that are widespread and could be heard at almost any occasion were: 'scrape some money together,' 'put some money aside,' 'a little nest egg.' These expressions mean that, by keeping a patient, the host families are able to earn money that they would not otherwise be able to. The State pays the host families only twice a year, so that they have the impression of receiving a large sum of money. Although most host families are well aware that they invest money in their patient every day for food and lodging,

psychologically speaking, they feel rewarded when they collect this rather large sum twice a year. The fact that many
host families asked the members of our team to do something
about raising these fees, which are no longer considered
sufficient, shows that boarding is seen as a means of financial
gain.

In former times patient care was certainly a way of earning
money, but then Geel was a village made up mostly of
farmers. Vegetables, fruit, potatoes, milk, butter, and meat
were all produced on the host family's farm. The amount of
money invested in a boarder was virtually nil, while the
patients contributed in the form of manual labor in the field
or in the household. Vermeulen mentions a few rare cases
where the patients had succesfully taken care of the entire
organization of the farm[3]. They decided what was to be
planted and sown, what labor should be done and when. At
one farm where the patient was closely involved with the
farm management, the choice of a new truck led to such a
quarrel that the patient had to be admitted to the central
hospital of the Rijkskolonie. Today, on the condition that
the farmer can get a 'good' patient, boarding is still considered a profitable business. A 'good' patient is someone
who makes little trouble, is reasonably quiet and manageable,
and is economically profitable by doing a lot of manual work
or by paying a high boarding fee. A patient, quoted by a
Geelian, expressed this in a picturesque and mocking way:
"A 'good' patient is someone who produces 25 liters of milk
a day, lays two eggs every day, and does not ask for pay at
the end of the week." The term 'a good one' is so widespread
in the colloquial language that there is no purpose whatsoever
in wondering what type of people use it. The expression is no
one's and everyone's, and throws unequivocal light on the
motivation of the host family as it is experienced in the
endoculture.

Some older members of former host families, no longer
involved in the system and able to talk more freely, told us
that there used to be some corruption and favoritism in the

placement of boarders. Certain district nurses arranged the placement of 'good' patients in exchange for small bribes. Sometimes a small amount of money was shoved into the patient's 'booklet,' which must be signed by the district nurse every two weeks. This was a discrete way of giving 'tips.' The traditional present used to be a ham. A host family that had seven patients told us that one of the nurses regularly came to the farm to have hams smoked and afterwards sold them. Also recently a small company's patient was withdrawn by the Rijkskolonie because the nature of the business had changed in such a way that the new business was no longer compatible with boarding. The host family claimed to have paid the nurse 15,000 BF ($375 at the time) in order to obtain a 'good' patient, and threatened litigation because the patient was taken away from them. Another ex-host family told us that there used to be a doctor at the Rijkskolonie who arranged for a 'good' patient under the condition that the applicant send his children to State schools and not to Catholic schools. We do not intend here to expose any former or present corruption in the system. We only mention these 'facts,' even if they be pure fantasy, because they throw light on the cultural image of the motivation for boarding.

Other facts indicate the predominance of the economic component. There is a widespread opinion in Geel, also current among the host families, that certain farmers exploit their boarders. In a bar, a young man, who was an active member of the Young Catholic Workers, told one of our researchers: "The farmers especially get a lot of profit from the patients. Many farms owe their wealth to the work of the patients. The farmer didn't have to do a thing and the patients, they worked for nothing. And it's still like that now.[4]" On many other occasions we heard similar remarks about the Geel system. We ourselves observed a few cases of such abuse. Sometimes the Rijkskolonie is forced to take action and withdraw the patient. Such withdrawal is a great disgrace to the family involved and these incidents are remembered for years. The extent of abuse cannot be determined, but there has been, and still is, exploitation. As indirect evidence to this we note that host families consider it honorable when medical examination shows their patients have gained weight. This means that the patient is well taken care of, and that he is given more food than work. In other words, increase in weight is evidence of nonexploitation.

That the Geelians themselves are convinced that boarding is primarily based on economic motives is shown by the host families' response to the following question: "Do you think patient care will survive in Geel?[5] " Both yes and no answers were based on the same line of thought: "The system will survive as long as it is profitable to boarding families; if it is not, it will die out."

Those who think boarding will disappear see things from the point of view of the host family that has stopped farming and for whom the boarder is no longer a helping hand. A person who is not a farmer has to buy everything in stores, so keeping a patient is more expensive. He does not gain anything from it and may even lose money on it. On the other hand, young women are offered work in factories that have been established in the Geel area. A woman can earn much more money by working in them, and there is no one extra to take care of after working hours.[6] The family's mobility increases. In addition, an extra room has to be provided when a house is built. The latter factor seems to play such a determining role that the local authorities have requested the government to apply special standards to Geel in granting building subsidies. This sober financial fact may indeed have a great impact on the motivation to take in a patient. If one wants to board one or two patients now, one may have to build a larger house, thus losing the right to building subsidies and requiring the payment of more taxes and a larger investment. All these factors are economic.

Those who think family care will continue base their opinion on economic motives as well. They argue that there are still many farmers who can use cheap labor, and that the demand for boarders is greater than the supply. However, one head of a host family observed that more and more farms are being mechanized, thus depriving the patients' labor of its primary meaning. The heavy work is done by machines and no one is inclined to put this expensive equipment into the hands of a patient. Moreover, an increasing number of patients have recently come to Geel who are not used to farm work because they come from nonfarming backgrounds. Hence, patients are becoming less and less useful. Some also add that patients nowadays demand more and more of the host family's time, because they should somehow be kept busy. Patients cannot sit around all day or they become unmanageable. In other words, patients become unproductive in a double way: They do not work anymore themselves and they require a greater investment of time by the host family. Finally, the therapeutic value of labor is disappearing.

Some hard sociological facts confirm these conclusions of 'folk sociology.' Boarding is indeed primarily connected with economics. With the vast majority, if not all, of the host families belonging to the lowest socioeconomic strata[7]. There are only a few exceptions: Some fairly wealthy farmers and families that have made a quick climb on the social ladder have kept their patients. People who consider themselves as belonging to the 'better classes' no longer take in patients. This segment of the population is growing. Geel used to be a relatively homogeneous community, with most of the income of the inhabitants based on farming. In this context, the patients were useful to almost everyone, even to the 'rich,' such as the notary, the doctor, the pharmacist, and other notables. They could afford to keep a patient to tend the garden without suffering a loss of status. The higher class at that time was so far removed from the rest of the population that the 'rich' felt no threat to their social identity by boarding patients. Everyone knew that these 'rich people' did not really need the family care arrangement. Industrialization, and the urbanization that came with it, led to growing differentiation of social positions[8]. This differentiation is also the product of longer schooling, which has resulted in a wide range of occupations varying from small farmer and unskilled worker to skilled worker, clerk, engineer, manager, and medical specialist. Today, patients are taken or kept almost exclusively by farmers and low-income level people, i.e., the people with the least amount of education. In this new economic context, boarding a patient becomes a symbol of 'needing it,' 'being less well-to-do,' and 'having no choice.' If this tendency continues, it may be feared that only those from the 'lowest' socioeconomic class who 'have not quite made it in life' and the small farmers who try to make it with the help of cheap labor will continue to be involved in family care. We shall return later to the implications of these socio-cultural changes in Geel. It is sufficient here to indicate to what extent the economic component is important to the system.

We may conclude from the above that economic gain, in the broad sense of the word, is an important aspect of the motivation for becoming a host family, and perhaps it is the only decisive stimulus. Patients are taken in because they are expected to yield a profit in one way or another. This motive is clearly recognized and formulated on the level of the endoculture, and no one feels they should be ashamed of it. On the contrary, everyone states that family care should be financially rewarding, and for years host families have been pleading for an increase in State subsidies. In this context it becomes perfectly clear that, to the Geelians, boarding a patient should not be praised as an act of Christian love. The congregation would only smile at the great naiveté of the preacher. So we can say that family care is business. But we must immediately add that it is not only business. The motivation to take in a patient unequivocally aims at financial profit, but the reasons for *keeping* a patient, once he has been adopted into the family circle, transcend economy. This is certainly true if it is considered on the level of ethical standards.

It has long been a custom in Geel that children simply take over a patient who has lived with their parents for a long time when the parents become ill or too old or die. This rule is not always observed[9], and if the children live outside of Geel it is even legally impossible. In other cases the children may lack room, both spouses may work, or there are other reasons that interfere with such transfers. But the rule still stands. A patient who has lived for years in a certain family becomes a part of it. If this is not the case, then something has gone wrong. The personal tie between patient and family cannot be broken without serious reason. Legally, of course, one is totally free; morally, one is not. Anyone who does not observe this code is criticized by his peers. In rationalizing this standard, people say that it means great suffering to the patient to be forced to readjust to a new environment after so many years. He feels that he has simply been thrown out.

Perhaps we touch here upon the heart of the Geel family care system: Age-old tradition has proved that 'normal people' can establish personal relationships with the mentally ill and with all kinds of 'deranged' persons, and that the tie is such that it seems immoral to break it. We may perhaps speak of some kind of 'structural,' built-in humanity or brotherly love. That the patient was initially taken in because the host family saw the possibility of gain and that the patient has been profit yielding does not negate this, nor do the abuses that exist here and there.

Without there being much theorizing, Geel ethics are based on the notion that every patient is a human being. This idea is often explicitly stated to outsiders. Moreover, it is reflected in the rule, which is generally observed, of never calling a patient 'crazy' or 'dumb.' This habit implies that one starts from a basic respect for the patient's humanity. However, as will be shown in the following chapters, this recognition of the patients' human condition is immediately corrected by considering them as a separate category, and thus keeping them 'in their place.'

Ideally, the patient is someone who, after the initial trial period, belongs to the family as one of its members. This implies that the patient is allowed to sit at the table and eat the same food as the other family members. The patient has to be lodged in a room in accordance with the standards set up by the Rijkskolonie. The patient should be allowed to stay when there are visitors and should be involved in family events to the extent of his ability. It is accepted that there may be conflicts, that the patient be given orders and the behavior regularly checked on, that the patient be taken firmly in hand and even disciplined once in a while. But it is absolutely not accepted for the patient to be ignored. People expect that the relationship (after years of living together) somehow becomes personal.

It would be very difficult, if not impossible, to determine reliably what feelings and relationships actually develop between members of the host family and the patient, or what concrete forms this relationship assumes in every particular case. If the host family is asked how things are, unreliable answers are obtained for various reasons. The same is true of attempts to obtain information from boarders, assuming this would be possible. On the other hand, it is impractical for a researcher to enter a large number of families and stay there. The only way of building on a firm basis in this matter is to assemble the reality piece by piece through empirical research based primarily on indirect evidence.

Although our research was not specifically aimed at this objective, we were able to observe that a large diversity exists in basic relationships between host families and patients. We noted a case where the mother of the family overtly stated that her patient was just a nuisance whom she would send right back to the Rijkskolonie if she did not need the fee. This woman claimed that the patient soiled her bed for a long time 'out of sheer stubbornness,' until one morning she pushed the patient's nose in her own wastes. Then it stopped. This woman told us that the patient was given only half a sandwich at night, preferably before 6 p.m., so as to prevent her from dirtying her sheets. The prescribed drugs were not given because they made the patient sleepy in the daytime and sleepless at night, which upset the boarding family's life rhythm. The host family emphasized that they did not enjoy the patient's company at all and that she gave them only trouble and 'filth.' To them boarding was a purely financial matter.

In another case, the patient threatened the family itself. The patient, a young, physically attractive woman, had tried several times to seduce the father of the family by presenting herself naked when she was alone with him in the house. The young family, which had four children, decided, after long deliberation, to keep the patient because her suffering threatened to become hopeless. She had already been transferred from four other places.

In other cases, we are certain that the boarder is nothing more than a cheap servant. There are also cases where the patients are full members of the family and participate, to the best of their ability, in all its activities. However, it is impossible for us to reconstruct the distribution of these relational types and their intermediate forms over the total family population.

Whatever the actual situation, the ethical standards of the Geel system give it a particular form and sphere. The fact that the boarder is not pictured by the endoculture as an object of charity or special compassion, together with the fact that fostering is clearly and explicitly viewed as a profit-making activity, creates a situation of normality. There is no preaching in Geel on behalf of the 'unfortunates' of the community, for such would make no sense. Associations do not collect money or organize events on behalf of the 'forgotten' minority that the patients of the Rijkskolonie would constitute. The patients of Geel are simply 'the people from the Kolonie,' a special kind of people with whom none of the Geelians identify themselves. But because they have always been there they are a normal ingredient of life, part of the landscape, and, at any rate, part of the social system.

The overall situation, however, implies that the unique Geel family care system is being threatened if boarding remains an undervalued occupation that lowers the social status of the host family.

NOTES

1. See, for example P. D. KUYL, *Geel Vermaerd door den Eerdienst van de H. Dimphna,* Antwerp, 1863.

2. See below, Chapter eight: "The Boarders and the Voluntary Associations."

3. J. VERMEULEN: oral communication.

4. KAJ-Katholieke Arbeiders Jeugd.

5. During some seventy extensive open interviews with host families by E. ROOSENS.

6. As of December 1978, the basic compensation per diem is 200 BF (about $7.00). This amount is increased if there are special circumstances, e.g., if the patient requires extraordinary care or if not productive. The compensation is linked to the official consumer index.

7. See table of professions below, Chapter five. On the economic impact of family care for the Geel region, see K. Veraghtert, De Geelse Gezinsverpleging als Regionale Welvaartsfactor (1795-1860). *Bijdragen tot de Geschiedenis,* 1971, pp. 3-30; F. KUYPERS and K. VERAGHTERT, Het Geelse Rijkspsychiatrisch Ziekenhuis: Een Micro-Economische Cel als Regionale Welvaartsfactor, In *Geel ...,* pp. 447-491.

8. See J. DUPRE, Economische Ontwikkeling en Industrialisatie, in *Geel,* pp. 288-307; A. PALS-GHOOS, *Sociologisch Onderzoek naar de Gevolgen van Industrialisering in een Rekonversiegebied,* Leuven, Sociologisch Onderzoeksinstituut, K.U.L., 1972, Rapport 1972/1973; Idem, Maatschappelijke Verschijnselen tijdens Industriële Expansie. In: *Geel,* pp. 311-314.

9. M.-R. D'HERTEFELT-BRUYNOOGHE, *Gezinsverpleginspatronen,* p. 44: More than half of the most recent host families (starting family care after 1960) started family care by taking over the patients of their parents. See also ibidem, pp. 43-43, p. 101 and Tables 4, 9, 13, 16, and 17.

Downtown Geel.

The patients' fishing club.

Chapter 5

THE OUTSIDE WORLD OF THE PATIENTS[1]

Present-day Geel is not a country village, a remote place hidden amidst the green fields, where mental patients live together with the other villagers in protective seclusion. True, for centuries Geel has been a village of mostly small farmers, but the appearance of this locality has vastly changed in the last 20 years. The Kempen, the region in which Geel is situated, has progressively been opened to the world. Today, many industrial plants are established along the main canal in Geel, some of them branches or subdivisions of multinational companies. Through the center of the town runs a wide, busy boulevard and its main street looks like that of any small provincial town. Around this center are grouped a series of 'villages' with specifically rural characteristics. Until a few years ago one of them, Bel, was a typical small, isolated village.

The 1,363 patients living in families are scattered over the entire area.[2] They are lodged with 1,007 host families, with

376 host families having two patients, always of the same sex. When we divide Geel into parishes, the host family distribution is as follows:[3]

  (1) St. Amands: 145
  (2) St. Dimpna: 189
  (3) Holven: 124
  (4) Elsum 58
  (5) Larum: 109
  (6) Ten Aard: 100
  (7) Bel: 32
  (8) Winkelomheide: 95
  (9) Stelen: 44
 (10) Oosterloo: 19
 (11) Zammel: 41
 (12) Punt: 40
 (13) Olen St. Jozef: 3
 (14) Eindhout: 3

Except for a few areas, it is very difficult to classify the parish territories as rural or semiurban (i.e., central) as many parishes include parts of the outskirts as well as of the town center. In order to sketch a reliable picture of the physical environment in which the patients live, we have classified, after empirical investigation, each one of the 1,007 host family homes as situated either in the semirural, semiurban center or in the country. Obviously, there were some borderline cases, but it is fairly safe to say that about half (538 or 53%) of the host families live in the country and the other half (469 or 47%) in the center or in semiurban areas. Thus, a substantial number of patients do not live in the country or on farms.

This ecological status corresponds very well with the occupation of the 1,000 host fathers:

Employees: 30 (3%)

Rijkskolonie employees: 22 (2.2%)

Retired employees: 4 (0.4%)

Retired Rijkskolonie employees: 8 (0.8%)

Manual laborers: 262 (26.2%)

Retired manual laborers: 152 (15.2%)

Farmers: 203 (20.3%)

Farmers/industrial workers: 91 (9.1%)

Farm-product salesmen: 2 (0.2%)

Retired farmers: 145 (14.5%)

Retired farmers/industrial workers: 11 (1.1%)

Shopkeepers: 60 (6%)

Retired shopkeepers: 9 (0.9%)

No occupation: 1 (0.1%)

Of the 1,000 host fathers, there are 203 farmers, 145 retired farmers, and 102 others who combine or have combined farming with a job in industry. These 450 host families are mostly located in rural areas. The large majority of the other host families live closer to the center of town. This means that there are hundreds of patients living in areas without markedly rural characteristics, i.e., in row houses along fairly busy streets. So far, this growing urbanization does not appear to pose any special problems for the boarders. As we shall see later, the Geel patients do not seem particularly attracted by the calm of the country districts. The center of the town and the places where things happen are much more preferred as destinations for walks.

In the framework of this extensive community with its differentiated structure, the patients are given as much freedom of movement as they can handle without becoming too disruptive. The district nurses, in consultation with the host families, decide in which activities the boarders will be allowed to participate. Not all can go unaccompanied into the streets. Some patients are capable of going out for a walk, but prove to be too noisy or uncontrolled to visit the movie theater or bars alone. In other words, there are categories of freedom of movement adapted to the patients' capabilities.

Not all boarders are able to participate in the community life to the same degree for psychomotor or psychosocial reasons. Moreover, many patients do not wish to go out, even if they are capable of doing so. Age and sex play a certain role in this. The table below shows that 621 boarders (45.6%) are 55 or older.

Patient age classes	
65 years and older:	350 or 25%
55-64 years:	271 or 19%
45-54 years:	263 or 19%
35-44 years:	263 or 19%
34 years and younger:	216 or 15%

And, socially speaking, women (385 or 28.2% of the patient population) cannot go unaccompanied to soccer games or bars as easily as can men. There are also differences in verbal communication skills or habits: 64 boarders (4.7%) do not speak at all, not even to their host families; 75 (5.5%) occasionally mumble a little; 289 (21.2%) answer when spoken to, but never take the initiative to speak themselves; 838 (61.5%) initiate conversations; and some 50 boarders (3.7%), according to their host families, talk too much. Thus, about 1/3 of the patients are hardly or not at all inclined toward verbal communication, even with their families.

These various factors—psychomotor ability, age, sex, verbal communication capacity, or habits—provide some explanation as to why all patients do not use, or are able to use, the opportunities available for participating in Geel community life or for going out into the world.

Patient contacts with the outside world center around a few periodic events: a visit to the baths and a medical checkup every two weeks, a movie on Sunday afternoons, a soccer game every two weeks during the season, walking and visiting bars on weekends, an excursion or a camping trip with the Rijkskolonie a few times a year, or visits by relatives at the host family home. These periodic outside contacts are supplemented by some small talk during shopping, walks in the neighborhood, visits to the neighbors, and watching television at night. When the host family has visitors, which happens quite often, the boarders are usually allowed to stay with the company.

Every two weeks the majority of the boarders (1,185 or 86.9%) leave the host family for a few hours in order to take a bath in one of the Rijkskolonie's bathing establishments, which are situated all over the Geel territory. On these occasions the patient's general state of health is checked and the necessary hygienic care is given by the Rijkskolonie staff. The patients are taken from and brought back to their homes by buses. Almost all the patients look forward to this bus ride, which is an opportunity for them to enjoy the company of the other boarders and the nursing staff. These bathing trips are an initiative of the Rijkskolonie and take place under the supervision of qualified staff members. Contacts with Geelians are minimal or nonexistent on these occasions. Only in the neighborhood of the baths do some patients make a quick run to a shop to buy candy or other small things.

When the patients are given the opportunity to go out unaccompanied on their own initiative, considerably fewer patients do so than participate in the organized outings. Only 433 boarders (31.8%) regularly go for a walk, and 45 (3.3%) prefer bicycle rides, for which they need special permission from the Rijkskolonie. Among the walkers, 176 (12.9%) go for a walk four times a week and 181 (13.3%) go only once a week. The others go even less. Hence, a daily walk would not serve as a form of therapy for the large majority of patients. Indeed, walks in the calm of nature are not preferred. Only 32 patients intentionally go to the woods or the fields, while 101 habitually go to the center of Geel and others prefer

places where things are happening: the railway station, con-
struction sites, the canals, and fishing ponds; 143 patients
walk around in the neighborhood without a specific goal.

It is clear that the streets of Geel are not permanently
crowded with Rijkskolonie patients, quite the contrary. During weekdays, their presence is sporadic and hardly notice-
able. Curious outsiders who drive through the streets of Geel
'to watch patients' usually return home disappointed. This
implies that the impact of the presence of the more than
1,300 patients is minimal as far as traffic and street life are
concerned. In this respect, there is no problem whatsoever
for the community.

The one place where the patients are most conspicuous
and in the largest numbers is the movie theater entrance on
the central square on Sunday afternoon. No less than 372
patients (27.3%) go to the theater regularly: 229 go every
week, 56 twice a month, 49 every month, and 10 more than
once a week. The Sunday afternoon movie is also designated
for the Geel children. The patients are seated on the ground
floor of the theater, the children in the balcony. Usually, the
movies shown are action and adventure movies such as cowboy movies or spectacular comedies. As the detailed description in the chapter will show, these visits to the movie theater
are for many boarders much more than just seeing a movie:
They are also occasions for boisterous company and activity.

After the movie, many boarders go alone or in groups to
bars in the center or in the outskirts of Geel. Sunday afternoon, after the movie, is the appropriate time for a glass of
beer or for several. As we shall see from the analysis of Geel
bar life, the patients visit only those bars where they feel at
home, i.e., places that are mostly patronized by working-class
or lower middle-class people. Practically no patients go to the
more expensive establishments nor to bars for young people.
Only some 30 boarders regularly patronize bars on weekdays.
This would not only cost too much for most patients, but it
would also be viewed as inappropriate behavior.

Sunday afternoons also provide opportunities for going to soccer games at least during the season. There are 193 patients (14.2%) who go to the home games every two weeks; 23 boarders (1.7%) accompany the Geel team to out-of-town games, usually in other fans' cars.

Even on Sunday afternoons, the time of the week when most boarders circulate in Geel, there is no inconvenience for other Geelians. At that time it is easy for an outsider or a Geelian, if they wish, to visit bars without meeting patients. In Geel there are 143 bars, and after the movie or the soccer game the patients disperse quite rapidly over the entire community. Incidents practically never occur.

Only once a year do many Geelians unavoidably meet the 'people from the Kolonie': during the period from New Year's to Epiphany. In many Belgian communities it is customary around this time of the year for groups of children to go from door to door to collect small change or candy. Many patients (260 or 19.1%) participate in these activities and view the matter as a source of income: 103 go singing in the neighborhood for one day, 70 for a few days, 22 for a week; and 3 for longer than a week. Others restrict themselves to a few hours. A few patients operate with the help of modern technology and instead of singing run a tape recorder, which they hide under their coats. This annual event is welcomed sympathetically by the average public. The fact that patients, like children, go singing, indicates that they belong to a special social category which we shall treat in more detail later.

As appears from what we have written so far, the boarders who are considered capable of taking walks unaccompanied are allowed to do so. They can go to movies, bars, soccer games, and church. They are given opportunities to behave like 'normal people' and, as we shall see in later chapters, there are many patients who on such occasions rarely, if ever, exceed the bounds of normal behavior, even if their behavior is slightly deviant and they are never quite taken seriously by the Geelians. Patients are allowed to do various things away from home that normal Geelians do as well, and in this sense two or three out of every 10 patients are involved in the local community in one way or another. This permission to act like the others can be considered a means of acceptance, a form of integration. It would, however, be a mistake to think that this implies equality between 'normals' and 'abnormals.' Although there is no outright prejudical stigmatization or segregation, the difference in status between Geelians and the 'people of the Kolonie' is maintained in all circumstances, albeit in a subtle manner.

This pervasive differentiation is most poignantly expressed in the field of voluntary associations where social life assumes a formal character. The voluntary associations of Geel, and there are many of them (87 Catholic associations alone), do not accept patients as members. In the meetings and activities of these associations no patients are present, except only the very exceptional and then only sporadically. Some patients (16 or 1.2%) are members of sports or music associations, and about 50 boarders are occasionally involved in some kind of association activity, helping at or visiting public festivities. In formal meetings, however, patients are never present. We feel that this matter is so important as a part of the Geelian technique of dealing with mental patients that we will devote a separate chapter to it. It is sufficient here to point out this aspect of nonintegration: Patients are not admitted into the formal social life of Geel.

On the other hand, some efforts are made to provide the boarders with their own associational life. The Rijkskolonie has founded a fishing club of which 82 patients (6%) are members. Besides this there are two clubs where boarders can go on Sunday afternoons. The *Klimop Club* is the result of a private initiative taken by people who are closely involved with patient care. Different kinds of social activities are held there, and nonalcoholic beverages and candy are sold. This club is regularly visited by 111 boarders (8.1%): 65 of them

(4.8%) go every week, 23 (1.7%) every two weeks, the others less frequently. Another official *Klimop,* founded by the Rijkskolonie, has had less success: only 41 (3%) boarders go there of whom 10 (0.7%) go weekly and 10 others twice a week. The others go less frequently. Comparing these figures with those for soccer games and bar visits, we see that the large majority of the patients prefer to go to activities not specifically provided for them and where they also meet 'normal' Geelians.

In daily life, shopping brings many patients in regular contact with the outside world. There are 545 boarders (40%) who do the shopping for their host families regularly: 132 (9.7%) do this four times a week or more, 172 (12.6%) twice a week, and 140 (10.3%) once a week. Shopping is considered a service, a useful activity. It takes place almost exclusively in the immediate vicinity, so that patients deal with shopkeepers whom they know. Shop conversation with patients is traditional in Geel. One out of every three patients, according to the host families, enjoyes conversing while shopping.

In the same category of contacts fall the visits to neighbors who do not have a boarder themselves: 269 patients (19.7%) regularly visit one or more neighbors. Nevertheless, these visits are not particularly encouraged by the host families because they fear the boarders tell too much about what happens in the family. So neighbors can rather easily refuse patients' visits if they wish. Still, the figures cited show that hundreds of families accept such visits. It is striking that 269 patients visit neighbors who do not have a boarder themselves while only 56 (4.1%) visit other patients at their homes—and this in spite of the fact that 898 boarders (65.9%) live in the immediate vicinity of other patients.

Like the neighborhood, the host family home is a privileged place for meeting outsiders. Of all the patients, 235 (17.2%) live with host families who receive visitors every week, 406 patients (29.8%) see family visitors twice a week, and 332 (24.4%) four times a week or more. According to their host families, 709 boarders (52%) actively participate in these visits, 294 (21.6%) only answer when spoken to, 128 (9.4%) remain reserved, and 213 (15.6%) keep entirely at a distance.

The host families with whom patients live or have lived are also points of contact for visits the patients pay outside the immediate neighborhood: 48 boarders regularly visit relatives and acquaintances of the host family, and 15 visit their former host families. Visits to other Geelians outside the neighborhood are exceptional.

In the same host family home the patients receive visits from their own relatives: 644 boarders (47.3%) receive occasional visits from one or more relatives, 198 (14.6%) from one or both of their parents, 38 (2.8%) from their sons or daughters, 443 (32.5%) from their brothers and sisters, 102 (7.5%) from their spouses or from other, more distant relatives. For 250 patients (18.3%), this is restricted to a once-a-year visit, for 231 (16.9%) this happens two to four times a year, 93 (6.8%) receive visitors five to 11 times a year, 60 (4.4%) every month, 8 (0.6%) every week, and 719 patients (52.7%) never receive visitors. This means that one patient out of two does not have any contact with relatives.

Most patients never leave Geel unaccompanied. But 190 patients (13.9%) are allowed one or several vacations with their own families, and the Rijkskolonie also organizes camping trips and excursions: 113 (8.3%) go on a trip once a year, 490 (36%) two to four times, 32 (2.3%) five to 11 times, and 121 (8.9%) participate in camping trips. Thus, interruptions in the patients' stays in Geel are limited, both in frequency and duration, as well as in the number of boarders involved.

The social network of the patients, which we have just outlined in a quantative and descriptive manner, will be analyzed more thoroughly in the following chapters. Nevertheless, it allows us to draw some conclusions at this point:

(1) The social relations pattern is not the same for all patients. The boarders' population can be divided into differ-

ent categories along a continuous line, going from boarders who never go out and do not speak at all not even to their host families, to very active patients who go for long walks every day, regularly visit bars, make contacts with neighbors, appear wherever things are happening, and regularly go on vacation with their own family without special accompaniment. From the therapeutic point of view, it may be important to note here that in Geel a wide scale of social interaction possibilities is progressively unfolded. Both the host family and the district nurse try to see how far they can go with a patient. The patient's freedom is restricted if he proves unable to handle it. Such experimenting is only possible because Geel has a psychiatric center (the Kolonie) that can intervene coercively if the patient deviates too radically. In a sense, it can be said that the patients are never promoted above the level of their 'competence.'

(2) Altogether the relational pattern of the more socially active patients is at most only slightly different from that of the average host family, at least if we limit ourselves to the territory of the Geel community. In varying degrees the boarders go walking, shopping, visiting, attend church, and visit bars. Only in the field of voluntary associations, where the local community manifests itself socially in a more formal manner, are patients not given the same opportunities. In the movie theater they are also segregated.

(3) The impact of the patients' presence on the Geel community is rather limited. Spectacular incidents in public are prevented by barring certain types of mental patients from family care. Furthermore, as we have noted, patients are only allowed to do what they can handle. For example, a patient liable to provoke traffic accidents is kept at home. Geelians or visitors in Geel do not encounter 'disturbing' patients wherever they go nor do they feel that they are in an uncommon situation. Nothing is further from the truth. As far as street life and life in public places and establishments is concerned, Geel is strikingly ordinary. Many boarders are undistinguishable from other passers-by. And even if boarders

are conspicuous by their facial expressions or their somewhat poor attire, they do not usually act peculiar or make a great fuss. At most they just look a little different, not quite like the others. All true Geelians know stories of patients assumed by outsiders to be 'normal' inhabitants, and conversely, amusing stories of healthy Geelians taken by outsiders for patients. On ordinary weekdays and even for the greater part of the weekends, conspicuous patients are quite rare.

(4) In Geel the mobile patients do not form a closed group. The figures cited show that the large majority of the boarders prefer to go where they meet 'normal' Geelians. Grouping among patients or the development of closed networks involving only patients are exceptional.

(5) In our opinion, despite great changes made in many mental institutions and the attention paid to the resocialization of mental patients, Geel remains a unique phenomenon. Although the intensity of professional therapeutic care is still very low, the mature calmness shown by the large mass of Geelians in dealing with patients and the opportunities for social interaction provided them in the context of a 'true to life' community are altogether very uncommon. Geel's great achievement is certainly that, in spite of the presence of more than 1,300 mental patients, it has remained such an ordinary community.

In this chapter we have tried to give a quantitative outline of the boarders' life in the Geel community outside the host family. In the following chapters we will approach these same phenomena in a qualitative way and discuss in more detail the actual form and content of the relationship between the patients and other Geelians. To this end we have chosen six typical situations: patients in the street, in church, in the movie theater, in bars, in voluntary associations, and in their intimate orientation towards others.

In Chapter 10, *Normal and Abnormal,* we shall consider whether these different situations reveal a constant pattern in the Geelian-patient relationship.

NOTES

1. The figures mentioned in this chapter have only an approximative value as the number of patients varied during the course of the study.

2. We use the present tense to refer to the time of our investigation, 1969-1974.

3. See also the map in this book. No data were available for five of the host families.

Street scene on a holiday.

The Geel Fair.

Chapter 6

BOARDERS IN THE CROWD

More striking than the fact that so many patients stay at home is that more than 400 boarders do indeed go out unaccompanied. In the majority of cases these are people who have shown themselves unable to cope or behave 'properly' in normal life. In a 'normal' village many would be stared at. One would expect them to be involved in a series of traffic accidents, to provoke incidents disturbing the public order, to commit a series of more or less serious crimes, as do the 'unbalanced,' maniacs or the sexually frustrated,—all the more so because another part of our investigation has shown that more than 16% of the boarders have obvious sexual problems. If we look back on several decades of home care, we see that such spectacular occurrences are absent. There are no sex murders and, according to the chief of police, Geel has a lower criminality rate than the surrounding communities. Of the 2,500 police warrants issued annually at Geel, only some 50 are related to Rijkskolonie patients. The chief of police expressed the wish that he would have as little trouble with the 'normal' population of Geel as with the boarders.

From the point of view of relational therapy, walking can be interpreted as a therapeutic activity[1]. The patients go out from the intimacy of the boarding family, come into contact with the outside world, and in a way, enter into society. They see other people, are themselves seen, and come into contact with nature or with the urbanized town center. In other words, they have a number of opportunities to enlarge their world of experience.

To the outsider it is striking that the patients are not stared at in the streets or watched in any special manner. The average Geelian accepts without question the patient who gesticulates, who dresses in an old-fashioned or extravagant way, who sits down on the sidewalk, or who talks to himself. Boarders have become so familiar that they are part of the landscape. In public there is no suggestion given to the patients that they belong to a special category of people. They are allowed to go everywhere like anybody else.

On the other hand, there are enough people around who will quickly react to imminent danger to, or change in, a patient. If a patient in the street suddenly becomes aggressive or unruly and creates a danger for passers-by or in traffic, the Rijkskolonie is called. When a female and a male patient are seen often together in a remote place, the case is reported. Without it being obvious there is comprehensive surveillance in Geel that provides for almost immediate intervention by the Rijkskolonie. This surveillance, done by 'normal' Geelians, is very discrete and has nothing in common with intensive supervision.

Unavoidably during their walks, or intentionally, patients encounter public events such as inaugurations and other festivities. On these occasions, when many members of the community are in the streets and function as an organized unit, the attitude of the Geel public towards the patients is most clearly expressed. In order to provide an idea of these interaction patterns between the ill and the 'healthy' in this context, we insert here a report from the field study[2].

"The October Youth Week starts with a parade of youth organizations through the center of town, followed by a mass meeting in the market place. A lot of people have come into town and, as every Sunday afternoon, dozens of patients are present."

"Many boarders have come to town on their own and stand more or less among the spectators. Some are accompanied by a few members of their host family and discuss the events that pass before them. Most patients, however, have come in small groups of three or five, and comment, loudly and with obvious gestures, on the different groups and marching bands."

"Three younger boarders march along with the band, on the sidewalk or behind the onlookers. They shout with excitement to each other, point to the instruments and follow the rhythm of the marching music with their arms. A middle-aged boarder, rather small in size, marches along with the band at the side of the road. He swings one arm with short and passionate movements, to the rhythm of the music; his other arm is tightly pressed against his body; with his head high and his chin in the air, he is a solemn but highly emotional figure. His face is set, as if filled with suppressed enthusiasm. His pace is short, and he swings the upper part of his body and his head in time to the music. This patient wears a very decent suit that fits him well. His tie is somewhat improvised, and on his feet he wears rather ponderous, unelegant shoes. He marches along with the band even with the drum major but at the side of the road, a bit ahead of the musicians. Sometimes he marches impassively ahead, then turns around and faces the players as if to conduct. This patient can be seen at many parades, always in front with the marching band. Sometimes he tries to march in the middle of the street so as to really play the bandleader. At those times, however, he looks shyly about him to see whether anyone who might stop him from doing this has noticed him. One move or word from the bandleader suffices for him to quickly resume his place along the sidewalk. There too, he glances about him once in a while to see whether someone is planning to expel him from this priviliged place. I have never observed this happening. In former years I have often seen this patient in the possession of a wooden flute or a uniform cap which he carries as a thing of great value under his arm. Thus, in their own specific way, the patients are involved in the parade: either a bit absentmindedly and retiring, or talking in groups and actively participating."

"During the show, which consists of different groups reciting, singing, and dancing, the boarders mingle with the spectators. Many watch and listen attentively in small groups or with friends or neighbors. A few are withdrawn and seem to notice very little of the event. A threesome half sits, half hangs on the sill of a display window of a clothing store on the marketplace. As on every Sunday afternoon they have come to the center from far outside of town. Apparently they have sought each other's company. They do not talk but sometimes they exchange glances and then stare straight ahead again. Directly in front of them a costumed participant in the mass play passes. They look him over from head to toe and follow him with their eyes as far as they can. One of them takes a packet of tobacco from his pocket and starts rolling a cigarette in a very clumsy manner. The result is a very thin cigarette. The others watch this effort attentively, but not one word is spoken."

"During the intermission, when the young Boy Scouts who have been watching start walking around in the marketplace, a few patients mingle with them. They walk from one talking and laughing group to another, watch with curiosity, and admire uniforms and musical instruments. No one shows any interest in them as they stroll along. Then a patient is given a

Boy Scout's hat to try on. Proudly he lets himself be viewed by bystanders, among whom there are a few other patients. A little further on a patient is briskly telling a story next to a drum while a few youngsters encourage him laughingly. But this attention is short-lived for the boys are already preparing for another performance. Another patient, heavily and sloppily dressed, with a confused look and open mouth, is greedily watching a group of youngsters who are busy with some flags. Nobody reacts to his staring request, and only disinterest is shown in the hope that he will go away. He continues to gape until the youngsters themselves leave."

"In the meantime it has started to rain and the crowd drifts off. Some patients take shelter against the fronts of houses or shops or under the awning of a bar. Others are told by friends not to get wet and to go home."

From the above, we may infer the following:

(1) One element (a constant in all reports of public events) is that the patients are present in different ways. The manner in which a number of boarders remain alone and isolated within the crowd is always striking. Another group of patients, their number being difficult to estimate because it always fluctuates, stand or walk in groups of two to four. These groups have very little verbal interaction. They are in each other's company, yet very little is said. A very small minority is hyperactive. These hyperactives are usually figures who are well known to the public and who always try to be in the public eye at such events. In the above report such extroverts are the 'drum major' and the few young people who march along with the parade. At all events of this type, a small minority—10 at the most—always tries to be noticed. The other patients, the majority, recede into the background, like 'normal' spectators.

(2) The report also shows that the Geel public tolerates the demonstrative patients' shows and pays little attention to them as long as the collective activity is not disturbed. If the situation becomes confused and one of the 'normal' specta-

tors feels threatened in his social identity and role, for example by a comic effect, then some member of the community reacts. Thus, for instance, a boarder is allowed to play drum major as long as he marches along at the side of the street. Everyone can see that he is imitating and is not taking the place of the real band leader. If, however, the boarder tries to reduce the distance between his imitation and the original model by marching in the middle of the street, there is bound to be a reaction and he is quickly put back into his proper place. The same sequence appears from a report of the opening ceremony of a large department store[3] : "At the opening of X, a new department store, an official ceremony was held. The day before, a commercial parade had gone through the streets of Geel. As with almost any parade, patients constitute a more than proportional part of the spectators. Those who are shopping or walking stroll around for a while in the vicinity of the marketplace; those who spend their days idling are present as well. Flyers and free samples are being distributed. More fervently than the children, the patients try to collect as large a pile of these things as possible. At the opening ceremony a few speeches are made, a ribbon is cut, and so on, while a crowd of curious and eager shoppers gathers before the entrance. A patient, who has come into town especially for this occasion, breaks loose from the crowd, walks over the rolled out carpets, and joins a group of leaders. He is very sloppily dressed and unshaven. He wears dirty wooden shoes, clearly, those he uses to work in the stables. A brief and slightly amused wave of surprise passes through the audience. The manager of the store glances disapprovingly at the patient, who does not seem to grasp the situation. But the ceremony continues, without anyone paying any particular attention to the patient. One of the store personnel has almost imperceptibly approached the patient, pulls his sleeve and leads him calmly and with silent admonition to a place among the spectators. A few patients have noticed the 'disturbing element' and

comment on the event with restrained laughter. The bystanders have apparently forgotten the incident and the ceremony
continues." As in the former cases, no one reacts to the
presence of patients in the audience. If, however, a patient
steps out to join the leaders, he puts himself in a place that is
in sharp contrast with his status and role in the community
and overturns the social hierarchy.

(3) The Geel public is not insensitive to the comic aspect
of an incident in which some patient creates a laughable
situation, but the incident is never exploited. The patients are
not encouraged to perform a kind of circus act.

(4) When a patient is publicly reprimanded, it is never
done in a blunt or brutal way. Spectacular interventions are
avoided and things are done discretely and gently. In this way
an attempt is made to prevent violent reactions by the
patient and at the same time a disturbance of the collective
event is avoided.

(5) The Geel public clearly sees the deviations in the
patients and makes no effort to conceal them. People act as if
they do not notice. This nonresponse to the patients' behavior—at least so long as it remains within certain limits—has
become their second nature: It belongs to their culture.
Everyone considers it quite normal that certain patients
behave somewhat strangely at public events. This does not
imply, however, that it is part of the therapeutic aim to erase
the differences between normal and abnormal behavior.
Nothing is further from the truth. As our study on the
interactional patterns in the bars abundantly demonstrates,
the border line between the 'ill' and the 'healthy' is clearly
drawn. But according to the Geelians themselves, experience
has proven that one should never react strongly to a patient
in public. Usually things get worse that way, and nothing is
accomplished.

The same characteristics of the interaction pattern
between the boarders and the 'normal' Geelians is found in
the Sunday church services, i.e., the Roman Catholic masses.

For the following report it is to be noted that even the children pay little or no attention to deviant behavior in church and do not make fun of it[4].

"The 10 o'clock Sunday mass is always attended by some 30 patients. Their presence is quite conspicuous because this service is not attended by a large crowd and the worshippers, usually regular attendants, are spread over a large area."

"Patient M is always early. He is very well dressed and has a large prayer book, which he usually appears to be reading attentively. He is French-speaking and does not participate in the Dutch service. He conscientiously follows the movements of the priest and the other people and responds accordingly."

"Every Sunday an old, stooped patient sits a little behind him. He usually comes in hastily, hunched up, through the nave. He is always late. He sits huddled up on a chair and remains like that throughout the entire service. In his rough, weather-beaten hands he holds a small prayer book, through which he leafs feverishly. After a short while his arms sink to his knees, his head droops, and he falls asleep. Awakened by the sound of chairs moving, he sits up again, resumes his reading, though not for long."

"In the left row, in the middle of the church, are three young boarders. They seem to be novices. They glance nervously around them to watch what the others do and try to follow what is going on. Sometimes one of them turns around and stares at the worshippers, one after the other. The congregation pays no attention to him and it is as if the three were not sitting there. The children, who are in the front rows, look at them from time to time, but apparently without much interest and certainly not for amusement."

"On the aisle, next to a pillar, huddles another patient. Immediately upon entering he sits down, crosses his arms over his chest, and falls asleep. His head moves with his breathing and from time to time he snores. Every Sunday he sits in the same place in the church and always in the same manner. Never have I heard anyone make a remark about him or react in any other way."

"In the middle of the church, behind the school children, sits patient F. He is very tall and looks around in all directions. He tries to follow closely what others do: kneeling, sitting, standing up. Sometimes he tries to anticipate certain movements, but is always late. Once he sat among the school children while wearing three watches on his arm. The entire service he spent manipulating and adjusting his three watches to the great interest of the children. The chaplain afterwards carefully helped him to understand that perhaps it would be much better to sit behind the children. Another day during a long sermon by the Pastor he stood up yawning, stretched out both arms, and sat down again. This, a very humorous act to outsiders, only surprised a teacher who had been living in Geel for only a couple of years. None of the many school children who were present reacted."

"In the back rows of the nave, close to the exit, are seated most of the patients. A few young patients have come in as a group and leave before the end of the service. Each one of them has his own characteristic bodily attitude and expression. Most of them seem absent-mindedly waiting for the service to be over."

"Up in front on the left aisle sits a patient known as 'the pharmacist': a very noble and well-groomed figure with white hair and a beautiful beard. He stands solemnly, his head high, and sits down only after everyone else has sat down. He seems to follow the events attentively and recites the common prayers a bit too emphatically."

"In the left nave area a few female patients. They are easily marked by their obviously out-of-style clothes and obsolete hats. They seem to follow the service zealously. From time to time they talk to each other and tell each other to take this or that position. One of them has a shopping bag full of prayer books. Several times she opens the bag, rearranges her collection, takes out another book, and starts leafing through it with ardor."

"One Sunday a visiting priest preached an ardent sermon at all the masses. A boarder who always sat beneath the pulpit attended mass for the second time at 10 o'clock, thus having already heard the sermon. He continually commented on the sermon: 'This he said before, too!' The constant repetition finally became too much for the preacher, who asked that the 'disturbing element' leave the church. At this, the patient promptly answered: 'This he didn't say before!' Restrained laughter went through the church, and this concluded the incident. The boarder kept silent for the rest of the service."

The only public event where the patients could act in an organized manner as a group used to be the procession of St. Dympna, held every year on the first Sunday after May 15th. About 10 years ago, this procession was abolished in the wake of the 'de-mythification' movement in the Roman Catholic Church. As is shown by the following report, groups of selected patients, whose behavior was entirely normal, marched in this procession along with others who were rather conspicuous.

"Ever since the procession on the occasion of the centenary, each year some groups, in addition to the usual groups in any parade, portray the life of St. Dympna in the procession. Models of the church and the Chapel of St. Dympna are carried along, followed by groups of penitents and pilgrims. These groups are made up entirely of patients. Very earnestly and modestly they stride along to the rhythm of the music. It is warm and, heavily clothed, they march straight and erect without turning their heads. It is apparent that they are very proud to fulfill this honorable duty. Behind the band a few boarders march as well. One of them focuses all his attention on marching in time to the music, and every time he fails. His friend tries to show him how to do it, but it is no use. A third one looks at the couple disapprovingly, pulls at the arm of one of the leaders of the band association and points to the 'disturbing element.' A sharp remark is sufficient to startle the two and they walk on in silence."

"Behind the monstrance, which is carried in turn by the dean and the parish priest, walks a small group of the faithful. About one third of this group consists of patients. Some follow, modestly, like the other faithful in the procession. Some walk arm in arm, and several look all about them while walking. No one pays any attention to their behavior, and most of the spectators are gone by the time they pass."

These field reports clearly show that the Geelians do not discriminate towards the patients as long as they are dealing with interaction of an impersonal nature and implying a minimum of mutual involvement. The only 'discriminating' element is perhaps that they tolerate more from patients than from 'normal' people and that the boarders' behavior is corrected if it deviates too much from the norm. Except for these restrictions, it can be said that boarders who go out in the streets are completely integrated into the community.

Things become different if the interaction pattern between boarders and Geelians implies more than just impersonal attendance at a public event. This is, for example, the case for movies. Officially, patients are not permitted in movies intended for adults only: they are only allowed to go to the Sunday afternoon shows for children, for which they need a permit from the Rijkskolonie. More than 250 boarders regularly go to the movie theater. As we mentioned above, it is the only occasion where so many patients can be seen together and where they manifest themselves in public as a separate social category. Team members were repeatedly told that if they wanted to see the 'people from the Kolonie,' they must watch in front of the movie theater on the marketplace on Sunday afternoons.

In the theater male patients are separated from female patients. The patients are seated in the lower part of the theater, the children in the upper part.

The Rijkskolonie authorities, who have created and still maintain this system, cite the following reasons for this:

(1) It is impossible for the only theater in Geel to show movies that attract both the patients and the other Geelians.
(2) Not all movies are appropriate for patients.
(3) The patients live the action of the movie so intensely that the show would become disagreeable to the rest of the audience.
(4) Men and women have to be separated in order to prevent incidents. That is also the reason why the children are seated in a different section of the theater.

A member of our team attended several movies for patients. Here follows part of his field report:

"Sunday, December 12, 12:30 to 4 p.m."

"Although the show starts at 1:30 p.m., the entrance hall of the theater is already filled with people at 12:45. Some patients stand at a distance, probably not wanting to be identified with the large group of 'oligophrenics.' I have the impression that the latter constitute the greater majority. Some patients pay for a ticket for a balcony seat. (A staff member told us that this happens frequently and that certain patients do this so as not to be identified with 'the people from the *Kolonie.*') Many patients in the hall carry transistor radios. Some display them ostentatiously."

"From 1:15 p.m. on more and more children arrive. Before, there were only a few standing together in a small group. Some are accompanied by their parents. A few host families also have come with their patients."

"On the main floor of the theater, which is reserved for the patients, who do not have to pay admission, there is a lot of noise. Only two children are sitting in this area. There is a lot of talking and running around going on, and the radios make a regular cacaphony. Even when the first feature starts (a Robin Hood film), the noise does not diminish substantially. It only disappears during the most exciting scenes when there is a fight or going to be a fight. Whenever the 'bad guys' take a beating, morally or physically, the whole house reacts turbulently."

"During the intermission the radios are turned on again and many patients go outside to smoke a cigarette. Many do this in the rest rooms where there is a crowd of people jammed together. Others watch the previews of coming movies or go upstairs to the bar. Most don't go in, but hang around at the entrance to the bar. A male patient is talking to an old female patient."

"Then the main feature starts. It is about Indians and soldiers. The reactions are similar to those during the first movie. Some are vehement. For example, when a soldier is struggling with an Indian, a patient shouts: 'Kill him! Kill him! Kill him!' Other reactions anticipate what is going to happen, for example, when the soldiers set an ambush to surprise the Indians."

"My wife had come with me to the show. She was sitting alone behind the crowd of patients. A boarder went up to her, sat down right behind her, left again, came back again, and so on. Finally, he asked her: 'Tell me, miss, would you dare eat worms like that Indian there?' And then: 'Miss, actually I would like to come and sit next to you, but I don't really dare to.' "

The following incident was noted during another movie:

"As always the women sit together on the far right. There are no more than 25. Most are older than 50, but today there is also a young woman of about 25. Some five men throw pellets of paper at her from the middle of the room during the intermission. Every time they throw one they all burst out laughing. But no one talks to the woman."

This report suggests that the reasons for separate shows for the patients are reasonable. In contrast with parades and other public events, watching a movie implies a level of mental development and self-control that these patients have not attained. On this point the integration of the patients into the normal public does not seem practical.

There is a consistent line running through the interaction patterns we have discussed so far: As long as the interaction between the Geelians and the boarders is restricted to passive common presence, as is the case with watching parades and other public events or during church services, we may not speak of a differentiating attitude toward the patients. But as soon as mental skills are required, a distinction or a division is made. This will become very clear when we examine two other typical situations in which the boarders communicate with other Geelians, namely, participation in bar life and in the activities of voluntary associations. As the expected interaction model becomes more and more personalized and involved, the relationship one has with patients diverges more and more from the kind that one would have with normal Geelians.

There is a danger that the reader who is not familiar with the Geel system may view these observations as moral evaluations. We positively wish to prevent such an interpretation. What we are doing here is only observing facts. We do not start from any conscious or subconscious ideal model of family care, expecting the normal participants to treat all patients without distinction as 'normal.' We leave it open here whether such a concept would be possible, assuming it were desirable. If the preceding observations, as well as the following, are nevertheless interpreted as a criticism of the Geel system, then this can only be due to a priori idealized notions about Geel. In that case this text can correct prejudice and stereotyping, which is, of course, the aim of any faithful description and scientific analysis of a phenomenon.

NOTES

1. Relational therapy as conceived, for example, by F. CUVELIER in *De Interaktie tussen Psychiatrisch Patiënt en Geels Pleeggezin,* and *Een Gastgezin als Kleine Therapeutische Gemeenschap* (see References).

2. R. BOUWEN, *Sociaal-Psychologische Studiegroep (Rapport Geel-Projekt),* 1, pp. 1-3.

3. Ibidem, 1, pp. 5-6.

4. Ibidem, 1, pp. 11-13.

The former site of the 'Klimop,' the patients' social club.

The author in one of the patients' favorite bars.

Entrance to the movie theater.

Chapter 7

INTERACTION IN BARS: THE 'JOKING RELATIONSHIP'[1]

The bars in Geel are regularly patronized by many patients. Going to bars is an excellent way to come in contact with the local community outside the family, and thus is an opportunity to enter into the larger circle of society. In bars they meet other Geelians and strangers. For this reason alone we thought it worthwhile to investigate how boarders are received in bars, what they do there, and how they interact with the bartender, the waiters and waitresses, and the other clients.

In addition, going to a bar implies a decision. Patients who have permission to visit bars unaccompanied have several possibilities open to them. They are free to go to these places. If they do, they can *theoretically* choose between a range of establishments ranging from select bars patronized by executives to the popular and poorly furnished bars where working-class people and farmers form the regular clientele. Theoretically at least, they have the choice between bars where people regularly dance and where the waitresses are the chief attraction, bars where there is a kind of family atmosphere among the customers, discotheque-type bars, exclusive inns where the local notables meet, or bars where mainly nonresidents go.

The choice of a bar can show us in which socioeconomic category the patients classify themselves or are classified by others; what patients can get and find in bars may throw some light on their environment; what they do there, what they are looking for, and how they are treated allows us to reconstruct one aspect of the patient's social identity.

In practice, we tried to answer the following questions:

(1) Can patients enter any bar, or do some owners refuse them admittance?
(2) What type of bar do the patients prefer and why?
(3) What can patients do in bars?
(4) What type of relationship with the other clients can they establish there?
(5) What type of social identity do the relationships in bars reveal?
(6) Does the actual situation give rise to abuse?

In order to investigate the happenings in the bars in connection with patients, we had to observe for ourselves without letting anyone know that we were observing. Since the Rijkskolonie forbade the serving of alcoholic beverages to patients a couple of years ago, it seemed to us that systematic interviewing of the owners would be interpreted as a kind of inspection. Moreover, it was highly probable that the modalities of contact with patients that did not conform to the ideal stereotype would be lost in the inquiries. Furthermore, we assumed that most owners would not be able to give an accurate and reliable description of the interaction patterns that normally develop between patients and other customers, even if they were willing to do so.

Thus, participant observation was the only way. While this technique allows close proximity to the object, it makes a statistically representative study impracticable. It is impossible to be present in the 143 bars in Geel at comparable moments of the same days during the week. One cannot wait for dozens of weekends, the time when patients mostly visit bars. If we had done so, we would have spread the investigation over a number of seasons, which in its turn would have introduced another uncontrollable and variable factor. In addition, such methods would have bypassed our objectives, which were not, e.g., to know within a certain timespan, how many times a patient was laughed at in how many bars. What we wanted was an understanding of the different types of bars the patients frequented and the various types of interaction that occurred. And this was perfectly possible with our method. W. Van Eyen, psychologist and anthropologist, was charged with this part of the field work.

For six weeks, from December 7, 1971, to January 16, 1972, 93 of the 143 official bars were watched from the outside to verify if patients were present and to judge their general character. Of the 93 bars, 43 were visited, some several times. On the whole, 106 visits were made, lasting from a quarter of an hour to several hours. All visits together took 4,680 minutes or 78 hours. Moreover, five Geelians who are closely involved with patients (four Rijkskolonie staff members and one of our colleagues, a sociologist) were asked to provide information on the bars appearing on the official list. Only reliable information was taken into account. In this way, information was obtained about another 36 bars. For various reasons, 28 of the 143 bars were excluded from the investigation, mostly because they were situated too far from the center of the town or were only open a couple of days a week.

The researcher's main task was to observe and record as accurately as possible the interaction between the patients and the other clientele. Special attention was given to recording the expressions (idioms) and the language used. The researcher was free to engage in conversation with the owners, the patients, and any other clients, if he thought this useful.

A very complex and nuanced picture appears from the field reports.

We shall first try to answer the following questions: "Can patients enter any bar or do some owners refuse them admittance?" and "What type of bar do the patients prefer, and why?"

One constant element observed is that only in exceptional cases are patients refused admittance to a bar *in a direct way.* Only one such case was observed and all conversations with bartenders, Rijkskolonie staff members, and the chaplain indicate the same thing: direct discrimination by refusing patients admittance to a bar is almost never practiced. (In the one case it was not clear whether or not this was an extraordinary incident.) The following text is taken from the field report.

"Sunday afternoon, January 2, between 5:30 and 6:30 p.m. The bar is mainly frequented by young bachelors. There is 'intimate' lighting and the customers regularly dance. The owner's two daughters attract customers. There are no patients present. A patient enters but immediately leaves again. One of the owner's daughters signaled him to leave. The two daughters (one about 25, the other around 20) serve as waitresses. There are only young people in their early 20s present. Occasionally the girls kiss and dance with the customers."

"During the second visit on Friday night, January 7, there are only three customers of the same type as during the preceding visit. No patients."

Though it is rather unusual to forbid a patient entrance to a bar, some owners use indirect means to keep them out, as shown by the following conversation and observations.

"Discotheque-bar. Green lighting. All customers are men between 20 and 30 years old. The wife of the owner and the waitress are very sexy. Sometimes people dance. Three young men are drunk. There are also some Tunesians, sitting by themselves. Conversation with waitress N: 'No patients come here. Sometimes one comes in, but we cannot serve them anything. Last Saturday there were four people from the Kolonie here. They sat at a table and asked for a 'beer.' They flirted a little—they were two men and two women—and one of them asked me: 'Is this allowed here?' [2] 'Oh, sure,' I said, 'Why not?' But when the boss had seen them drinking he said: 'Don't give them any more beer.' - 'Why not?' I said, 'They asked for it! Why should I refuse?' - 'Because they are from the Kolonie,'' he replied. I thought: 'Do they really come from the Kolonie?' I couldn't believe it. One of the girls who sometimes comes to this place wore a nice coat and slacks and I really intended to ask her where she had 'stolen' it—it was so nice! I could not believe those people were from the Kolonie.' "

In another bar where mostly young people meet, the owner said: " 'Yes, some patients do come here. But I've changed as far as those things are concerned. We still have four regular ones. In the beginning, when I started the bar, some years ago, I was so stupid! I felt sorry for them and gave them beer for five francs. You should have seen that! After a couple of weeks it looked here like the Rijkskolonie's cafeteria! The place was full of them, all day long! That was too much! (laughing) Yes, we have managed to get the fools out. We only serve beer to four patients anymore. If another one comes in, he doesn't get beer from us. You never know whether they can stand it. One day we had one who was already drunk when he came in. And afterwards he got beaten up in front of the bar. If the Kolonie would ever know that!'- 'Aren't they allowed to drink beer?'- 'Well . . . it's not a law. . . . As a matter of fact, you have to judge for yourself. To some of them you never give beer and to others you do. That's why we don't serve beer to patients we don't know.' "

From this conversation it is apparent this owner does not appreciate the visits of too many Rijkskolonie patients. The way to keep them out is to refuse to serve them beer. One can always refer to the Rijkskolonie regulation, but everyone knows that it is rarely applied and that there are no risks in serving in moderate quantities. The bar owned by the second interviewee is still visited by a restricted number of boarders.

In other places, patients are literally 'stared out,' except for some regular customers who, because of their particularly good relationship with the owner or with the other customers, have acquired some rights. This seems to be the case in some 10 bars, which are mainly visited by younger people. However, in such places there is little or no interest in the patients. The few patients who visit these bars are regular customers who for one reason or another, feel comfortable there and are accepted as individuals. This does not mean that there is overt discrimination towards other patients; people simply tend to make patients feel uncomfortable there.

A patient who very often goes to bars and who has been accepted among the few regulars in one bar for young people but is unwelcome in others says: "I come here very often because they leave me alone here. You are allowed to do what you like. In other bars, such as 'S' and 'N' (also mainly frequented by young people) people stare at you and make you drink. You should see them writing down everything you order and so on. That's why I never go there!"

In still another bar for young people, where patients are not attracted at all, the bartender tells us: "No, they don't come here. Many of them come and look in the door, but they don't come in. From time to time one does. But I don't know him, and I don't know if there are others. If you want to see them, you should go to the movie theater on Sunday afternoon." Through a reliable informant we later heard that the owner does not like the visits of patients because it could harm her business. She thinks her clients do not appreciate sitting with sick people.

As mentioned above, a restricted number of patients are accepted in some of the bars for young people. Either they are 'professional drinkers' who keep in the background or very popular 'characters' who seek out the company of youth and are tolerated because their presence does not have a disturbing effect.

"Bar N. almost exclusively visited by young people between 17 and 22. It is one of the most popular and the best decorated discotheques. Friday evening, December 10, between 10 and 10:30. Many young people, no patients. Sunday evening, December 12, between 9:30 and 11: the same. Monday evening, December 20: some young people, no patients. Wednesday afternoon, December 22, between 3:15 and 4: a small number of young people and one patient. The patient stands at the bar and occasionally teases customers or simply says: 'See you!' He gives most girls and some boys who pass by a friendly pat on the shoulder. Some of the young people react and make some gestures. The patient himself is deaf. He makes fun of the clients around him. Most of the young people, however, act as if they do not see him, not even when he gently taps them on the back. The patient tries to sell a packet of tobacco. He points to some young people and clearly shows them that they are very rich but stingy. The bartender: 'He comes here every day if he can.' Tuesday evening, December 23, between 8:30 and 9. Many young people, no patients. Sunday afternoon, January 2, between 5 and 5:30. Conversation with another patient, the only one present among many young people. He is between 50 and 60 years old. He says he comes from a town in Flanders, has had 6 children and a very good job. He says his children have all died. He says that one day when he was short of money he received 3 glasses of beer from the bartender. He says he likes to be among young people because the atmosphere is nice and happy. He behaves towards them exactly as the other patient who regularly comes here, tapping them on the shoulder and admiring the beauty of the girls. Many young people seem to know him, but they only say 'Hello!' or 'How are you?' No one starts a conversation. When I asked him where he lived, he asked me first not to tell it to the other people. Then he told me that he lived with a nice family who had taken him as a boarder."

"Saturday afternoon, January 8, between 3:15 and 3:45: a single patient, the first one mentioned, and some 15 customers. The patient moves over to someone who is playing a pinball machine and shouts advice to him. The other one nods but does not pay attention to the patient. Some time later, the owner winks at the patient and asks him by signs to buy 10 candles for the bar. The patient leaves the bar. Conversation with the barkeeper: 'J. seems to be a regular customer here?' - 'Yes, he is the best man we have.' A young man of about 20: 'He used to come here every day, but since he was sick, he doesn't come here as often anymore.' - 'The customers make fun of him?' - 'Well, sometimes.' - 'Do others come here?' - 'There was another one who came regularly, but he was killed in a car accident.' "

This report clearly shows that only a few well-known patients have been accepted as clients. They are mainly patients who try themselves to come into contact with young people. Subjectively, they seem to take much pleasure in doing so, but the young people generally take a passive attitude and do not bother with the presence of these traditional characters who have become part of the background.

"In another bar, frequented mainly by young people and a few older lower middle-class adults, we found a number of patients among the regular customers. There is a single patient who is in the bar practically all the time. The owner is rather young, and during weekends young people come help him tend the bar. Four visits were paid to this place and each time only the same patient was present. The patient told our researcher: 'I come from K (a large town) and I have been living in Geel for nine years. I like all modern things. That's why I come here.' Conversation with the bartender who is a student: 'Yes, there are some patients visiting this place, but they are not all fools, you know! Usually they can't do much about it themselves. For example, if their parents do not get along very well.' "

"During another visit we see the same patient again. And the next day between 8 and 9 p.m. he is there again. There are many people in the discotheque. The patient sits at his same place at the bar again. On both sides of him there are other clients. He does not talk to anybody, and nobody talks to him. When I enter I greet him and he greets me, but he does not show that he wants to have a conversation with me. Conversation with the same bartender as above: 'Is P from the Kolonie?' – 'Yes, but he's not a bad one, you know!' – 'Did he come here before the place was organized?' (In the past the bar was a meeting place for young drug users.) – 'Yes, every day the bar is open, he's here. That is, every Friday, every Saturday, and every Sunday from 7 p.m. on. He is always the last one to leave when I have to close up. He always asks for beer without a head. That way he always gets a little more beer and he can save money on the next drink. He always listens to the Flemish broadcasts of Radio Moscow. But I've told him once that it is thanks to our society that he can come here to sit and listen to the music and to drink. He had to admit this was true. One day he brought a scale model of a radio tower he had received from Russia. It was sent to him from Russia along with a letter that he showed to me!' "

"The next evening between midnight and 1:30 the same patient is there again. He sits at the same place and taps his fingers on the bar keeping time to the music. Sometimes he nods his head. Nobody reacts to this because everybody is allowed to do the same thing in this type of bar. A bit later he behaves very comradely towards some customers. They are three young fellows whom the bartender tells us are troublemakers who used to come here when the bar was a place for young drug users to meet. The owner plans to refuse the three young men drinks so that they will not come back. Once the patient talks to one of them, on a bar stool, arm in arm like two drunks."

This bar, too, seems to be visited by only one patient. The owner says that sometimes there are three others as well. The regular one seems to consider the bar a second home. He holds a fixed position there, but comes only occasionally into contact with other customers.

Apparently patients rarely appear in bars for young people. The clients don't bother with them and the owners have an indirect way of telling them that they are not wanted.

Patients do not go to some of the more exclusive places either. One of these bars is located in the center of Geel, two others are outside the town. But even the most exclusive establishment has not remained hermetically closed to Rijkskolonie patients. One patient regularly used to come there to demonstrate his talents, and he still visits the bar from time to time, though he does not live in Geel anymore. This patient was very good at mental arithmetic and could give the day of the week of a particular year for all dates. He only performed for money. Another patient still regularly comes there and feels quite at home with the personnel. He can hardly be considered a client, as the following report shows:

"A select bar in the center of Geel. Wednesday afternoon, December 22, between 1:45 and 3. We are the only customers (i.e., the researcher and his wife). At about 2:15 a patient enters and sits down in a corner near the window. Neither the owner's wife nor the waitresses react to his arrival. The patient sits down to rest a little and regularly looks at his watch. He stays there for about a quarter of an hour. When the waitresses start drinking coffee together with the two cooks, the patient starts making noises. One of the waitresses reacts by saying: 'Oh yes, S, we forgot about your coffee. Come and join us.' He goes and sits with the other people and is given a large mug, probably filled with ordinary coffee. The others drink filtered coffee. They tell a few jokes at his expense, but I cannot follow most of them. When they laugh, he laughs too. They seem to have a lot of fun. They ask him to show them his new watch. Then the patient starts caressing the arm of one of the waitresses who is a little bit plumper than the other. He stays in his chair. He seems to enjoy this and does it in a teasing way. The waitress lets him do it. The other waitress says: 'S, you don't do that to me, do you? But I know, my arms aren't that soft and chubby. Come here (to one of the cooks), will you caress my arm?' S teasingly caresses the arm of the waitress two more times. Everybody seems to enjoy this very much."

"Afterwards one of the waitresses explains spontaneously: 'That's S. He does the shopping here. Every day, in the morning and in the afternoon, he runs errands for us.' "

The two patients in this bar are not normal clients. The first one is an attraction and the second one is a kind of errand boy. One of the personnel informed us that some clients do not appreciate the presence of the first patient.

The fact that patients of the Rijkskolonie do not visit these 'establishments for the rich,' and are not welcome there except for a few exceptional cases and under specific conditions, clearly indicates their socioeconomic status. They are considered as belonging to the lower class of small farmers and manual workers with whom they board. The richer people rarely tolerate patients in places where they socialize. High social status and social contacts with patients are incompatible.

The last category of establishments where patients do not go, because they are simply not allowed in, are brothels. A well known brothel, now closed, refused entrance to all patients. Another similar establishment adheres to the same policy—probably because patients do not fit into this environment and because the owners fear trouble with the Rijkskolonie.

Without giving statistical value to the following figures, we think it is not mere chance that on 33 visits where patients were found, this happened 29 times in a popular bar. These are places frequented mainly by small farmers, lower middle-class people, and manual laborers, in other words, people belonging to the same class as the host families.

The existence of this general tendency, a preliminary conclusion of ours, was confirmed by our informants. Patients prefer to go to 'democratic' bars, because, as we shall see later on, they feel socially and economically more at home there, and because they are accepted into the company, albeit according to specific rules.

One of our informants (a district nurse) added: "The patients who, because of a better education, belong to a higher social level cannot go to bars where they would socially belong."

This first series of visits taught us which bars patients go to, and we have suggested some reasons for this.

By means of a series of more detailed case studies we shall now attempt to show what the patients can do in bars, what type of relational patterns they can establish there with other clients, and what type of social identity the patients derive from these relationships in bars.

In order to enable the reader to judge the material on which our conclusions are based, and in order to preserve the evidence of the interaction, we shall insert the reports of various observations carried out in different bars. We have chosen the cases in such a way that in each there is a different interaction pattern between the patients and the 'normal' clients. We want to stress once more that these cases are statistically not representative. However, they do show situations and interaction patterns in which patients can engage, possibilities that are offered to them, and how things really happen.

First, we shall reproduce the cases as accurately as possible, then we shall try to analyze the overall situation.

Case 1

In this case a family atmosphere dominates the relationship between the patients and the other clients. Patients can participate in the conversation as far as their capabilities allow. They are not isolated and are not in any special way encouraged to drink. They are accepted as peers of a special category without their illness being emphasized in front of the other clients. No one laughs at them.

"The bar is frequented essentially by workers and small farmers. There seems to be a rather restricted number of regular clients who hold apart from people they do not know. They spend their time talking, playing cards or pool. Sometimes they dance. The woman owner dances too. By her behavior she brings a kind of family atmosphere into the bar."

"Saturday evening, December 11, between 4:30 and midnight. There are two patients, A and B, and about 15 other customers. A is sitting at a table and B is sitting at the bar. Both of them drink beer. A has been playing soccer that afternoon and proudly shows off his shoes. Sometimes somebody speaks to him, but most of the time he initiates the conversation himself. The clients react sympathetically. Sometimes they smile at him, but they do not make fun of his behavior nor of his almost incomprehensible reasoning. B, who is, like A, about 25 to 30 years old, sits all the time at the bar and does not say a word. Nobody talks to him but he seems to follow everything with a vague smile. At 9:30 A asks B to accompany him. They leave the bar together."

"There is a family atmosphere in the bar. There is an old lady and a young family with a baby. The baby is passed from hand to hand. Some people play pool. Many of them are relatives: the owner, her brother, and her father, who is over 80."

"Sunday evening, December 26, between 8:30 and 11. The same two patients and an ex-patient (C) are present; there are about 10 clients. Patient A is playing pool with three other clients when we come in. B sits at the bar and sometimes talks to one of the clients. He talks mostly with the ex-patient. Both are drinking beer. They are treated but do not reciprocate. After a while they both become slightly drunk. B

speaks all the time about the big money he earns at the
farmer's place. He says this only to the ex-patient. Every
month, he says, he receives a new suit. He goes out very
often. He says he regularly visits the N. (a discotheque),
where he stays for many hours. He stresses that on New
Year's Day he won't go home before 7 in the morning. At
8:30 both patients leave and after 10 minutes come back
with french fries. The ex-patient says: 'Those two are
patients; you wouldn't say that, would you?' Some time after
11 they leave. When A pays, he holds the woman's arm and
smiles at her. Nobody laughs at the patients."

"After the patients have left, the owner tells us: 'I have
been here for about a year. Before that, I kept another bar,
the Z, for about 10 years. Last year a large group of patients
used to come with girls.' - 'With girls?' - 'Yes, you could call
them ladies. They were patients. But you couldn't see that.
They were dressed like you (pointing to my wife) and I. They
came here and danced. That was something! You must be
able to manage them. I can. One day one of them made some
trouble. He took a small amount of money from another
patient. From then on they were not allowed to come here
anymore. And the thief was punished. But that was not right,
really! They should have punished the other one, too. If they
can't keep their money in a safer place they should be
punished. Since then not many patients come here. Only
those two. Those who have to be home at 5:30 (p.m.) do not
come here. And the others actually aren't allowed to drink
beer. But when they have 9 francs, you can't say they're not
allowed, can you? Those two come here regularly. No, the
people don't bother about them being here. And anybody
who can't stand them, better stay away. They only come on
Saturday and Sunday. They don't come during the week.' "

Case 2

The second type of interaction we want to describe is
completely different. In this case the patient is publicly

treated by the bartender as a fool. Moreover, he is clearly sexually provoked and teased. Everybody present knows that none of these sexual invitations will be granted. This bar is not a brothel. The bartender is married and her husband is present most of the time.

"A plain bar, clients belonging to the lower middle and working classes. Sunday evening, January 2, between 8 and 11. One patient and two other clients. The patient drinks sweet ale. He talks a lot. He tells the owner and his wife and us that one New Year's day he went out singing with his guitar. He earned 1,200 francs ($30), he claims. In the course of the evening he will continually brag about the money he has. He says he is going to buy a new guitar and an amplifier which will cost him 7,000 francs ($175). The owner's wife doesn't believe him and writes on a piece of paper what each of these items costs. The patient turns out to be right. Three times she repeats that she is surprised that he has so much money. Then she whispers to us: 'This is my faithful Sunday customer.' "

"Sunday evening, January 16, between 8:30 and 9. There are about 15 clients, a very heterogeneous public varying in age and social standing. According to another collaborator on the Geel Project, who accompanied me, there was an ex-prostitute among them, who had worked in a well-known brothel in Geel. There are a few young couples and some middle-aged men. The same patient sits at the bar between two men of about 18. When we enter, the wife greets us from behind the bar. She asks: 'What'll it be, dears?' She does exactly the same when three other customers enter 15 minutes later. While we are there, she talks exclusively to the only male patient present."

"He must have patted her on the bottom before we came in. From behind the bar she says teasingly to the patient: 'You gave my ass a concussion damn it!' She repeats this a few times and then says: 'You don't believe you gave my ass a concussion! Look!' She lifts her dress in front of the patient, so that everyone at the bar can see her panties. Later on she starts again about her adventure with the patient. She says, while moving closer to him: 'C, there is something you don't understand! The customer is king but not in the owner's private rooms.' Supposedly C had followed her into the owner's private rooms before we entered. Each time C shouts back to show that he is not afraid of her and dares her to fight.''

''After having talked for a while about other things, the lady manages to change the subject in such a way that she can talk again with C about sexual matters. 'It is possible from behind, and it's fun too!' - 'It isn't possible!', C shouts. 'With a bull and a cow, yes.' - 'Well, aren't you a bull, C!', she tries. - 'Yes, but there's a difference!' - 'There isn't any difference. Come on C! It is possible and it's fun! Isn't my bottom good enough? Look!' She turns her back to C and lifts her dress again. 'You see,' she continues, 'I don't want any children. That isn't good for a business woman. But if it happens from behind I can always run away, you see?' - 'But . . . but . . . but. . . .' (The patient sometimes stammers) 'If you have children they could work for you in the bar. That's practical!' - 'Shit!', she shouts back, 'they only make trouble!' ''

''Then, in order to show that it is possible to have sexual intercourse in this way, she shows a sheet of paper, first to C and then to the other customers. It passes around the bar. There are some traffic signs on it. Sexual parts are represented in such a way that each drawing can be interpreted as a normal traffic sign. C, together with a couple of other customers, has a lot of fun with these drawings, though he doesn't make any comment.''

''When we prepare to go, the lady bartender shows surprise at our leaving so early.''

Case 3

In the third interaction pattern the patients are mocked as in the second. Apparently they serve as attractions and amusement to strangers. There is some talk about sex, among other subjects, but in a much more neutral way. The woman bartender does not make sexual allusions to herself; she only teases, and is not aggressive or defiant.

"Sunday afternoon, December 12, between 4:15 and 5:15. An old bar outside the center of Geel. Badly furnished and decorated. The woman bartender is about 30 years old. There are three patients, no other customers. One of the patients (A) has a hump and a crippled leg. He sits down and lays his leg on a bench. A second patient (B) sits on the chair near the stove. The third patient (C) sits at the bar. When we enter, the bartender leaves her chair near the stove and goes behind the bar. The only other customer comes in a quarter of an hour later and leaves almost immediately."

"Patient B talks about all sorts of things which are unintelligible to outsiders. The bartender regularly interrupts him and asks him questions meant to ridicule him in front of the strangers. She says: 'Oh yes, B, do you see colors in your room at night?' – 'Yes, fantastic! Blue, brown, and red. And they start spinning . . . and. . . .' – 'Don't you see naked girls from time to time?' B acts as if he were angry and turns his back to the bartender. 'Oh no,' she corrects herself, 'it's true, you only see the Blessed Virgin, don't you? But this C here, he's got pinups in his room, naked girls. Isn't that right, C? Let C have his naked girls! B will give them clothes, won't you, B? Because you've never seen the Virgin naked, have you? No, she always wears something!' "

"After a while the hunchback goes to the bar with some money in his hand and pointing to the jukebox he asks: 'Music . . .? Stereo . . .? How much is it?' – '150 francs!', the bartender shouts. – 'What!', he shouts back, and he gives her five one-franc coins to change. The bartender turns to us and says: 'You can bet he damned well knows how much it is!' Once he has the five-franc coin, she says: 'Look at him, what a sweet little face.' The man cannot operate the jukebox and remains in front of the machine until one of us helps him."

"When the music is playing, the bartender asks B if he likes it. 'Oh yes,' he says, 'I love all kinds of music.' – 'Do you like Will Tura too?' – 'Oh yes, and I like Marva!' – 'Are there any others you like?' she asks. 'Van Himst, for example?' – 'No, he isn't a singer, he's a soccer player!' – 'Oh yes,' she says, pretending she didn't know."

Case 4

The fourth case concerns patients in a bar where there are many people. There is dancing. In contrast with the preceding situations, there is not only much talking and teasing, but there is some erotic contact between the patients and other 'normal' customers.

"A bar in the rural part of Geel. The customers are working-class people and small farmers. People regularly dance there on Sunday nights."

"Sunday night, December 12, between 9:30 and 10:30. People present: the owner, his wife, their daughter (about 16) and a waitress (19), three patients and some 30 customers. They are of various ages. The girls serve the customers and dance very often. They are dressed in miniskirts. The three male patients are middle-aged."

"The three patients drink beer. A and B are a bit drunk. They don't drink much while we are there. As we entered, A stood at the bar, B sat at a table drinking beer in the company of a young man, and C sat at another table."

"During the evening A and B in particular mix with the other customers. C frequently dances: seven times in one hour. He dances five times with a middle-aged lady who sits at his table, and he dances two times with the 19-year-old waitress. He looks rather taciturn, doesn't talk to anyone, and always returns to the same chair."

"A remains at the same place at the bar. From time to time, however, he talks to people sitting at the table, who then laugh at him. Occasionally he invites a young girl (about 17) to dance, but she ignores him. B keeps asking the 19-

year-old waitress to dance, but she refuses. During the evening B dances three times with an elderly lady and once with the owner's daughter. When we entered, he was sitting with a young man at a table. Later he sat at two other tables and stood for a while at the bar."

"At one point two people sitting at a table are teasing A. They laugh at the kind of trousers he is wearing. A doesn't understand the mockery, and the more perplexed he looks the more the others laugh. He doesn't seem angry. Somewhat later somebody runs off with A's hat. A runs after him while the same group of customers laughs. At another time the jukebox stops and none of the dancers seems to be willing to pay for another record. Then the owner calls to one of the patients: 'Come on, B, five francs!' Some customers repeat these words. The owner's wife, who is sitting at another table, says: 'Come on, B! You collected money this afternoon so you can afford it!' And she continues to the people sitting at her table: 'He never sang in his life like he did this afternoon!' B goes to the bar and extends his hands to the owner's daughter for five francs. She refuses. Then another customer starts a record."

"Some time later B gets involved in a conversation with two other customers, one of whom is slightly drunk. During the discussion the owner's wife, who is sitting at the same table, continually interrupts B, saying: 'Don't shout like that, B, we aren't deaf!' Suddenly a man who has drunk too much shouts: 'But you are a patient, B! You are a patient!' To which B immediately replies: 'Yes, I am a patient but you, you are a fool!' And they continue their discussion."

"Up to now, B has tried several times to dance with a 17-year-old girl, and each time she has made an ugly face and teasingly acted as if she were afraid of him. Right after her last refusal a young man of about 20 invites her to dance and she accepts. From the middle of the dance floor she laughs mockingly at B who is watching her. He doesn't say anything and remains at his place at the bar. None of the other customers shows any reaction."

"After three refusals B finally manages to dance with the 19-year-old waitress because the owner's wife intervened and shouted that the waitress had to accept a dance. Although the girl shouted back that she was not allowed to do so by the owner, she begins to dance with B. After a few seconds the owner's daughter comes from behind the counter to B, hands him a beer mat and takes over his partner. B only says: 'Damn it!' and returns to the bar. After the dance, during which both girls have made themselves quite obvious, the owner's daughter returns to her place behind the bar. 'I won't forget that, N!', he says. Nobody reacts. Some minutes later B invites the girl to dance. First, she refuses, but then comes back and invites B herself, apparently to make up for what happened. After this dance, during which B seems to be in seventh heaven, both move to the jukebox where B puts in a five franc coin for another record."

"At a quarter past eight the owner's daughter tells B that it is time to go home. B is preparing to leave when the girl calls him back. According to her, he has not paid for the last beer. He pretends he has. She asks her mother, who says he has to pay. After some objections, he pays but looks really wronged. I asked the girl if he didn't want to pay. 'No, he didn't,' she says, 'and it's the same story every Sunday.' "

Case 5

Although many barkeepers think of patients as sources of revenue, just as they see other customers, there are some bars in Geel that are known to encourage the patronage of patients.

In the case that will now be described, there is no fraudulent exploitation of patients, but bartenders try to be as friendly with them as possible and they occasionally encourage patients to drink if experience has shown that the patients concerned can hold it.

In contrast with lots of other barkeepers, the owner and his wife in this case talked very freely about all kinds of patients who were part, or had been part, of their clientele. The researcher found it more difficult to stop the conversation than to start it. We give here his complete account because the bartenders' style and expressions make their attitude towards patients unequivocally clear.

One gets the impression that the bartenders use, to some extent, their familiarity with patients in attracting new customers. As will appear further on, patients in this bar are not integrated into a broader social context by meeting a familiar group of nonpatients. The main attraction seems to be the owner and his wife who pamper the patients and allow them to drink. The function 'drinking place' is primary here.

"A bar where mainly lower middle-class and working-class people meet. They are mostly lone men though there are also sometimes middle-aged couples. The owner and his wife are very friendly with the researcher."

"Monday evening, December 20, between 9:30 and 12:30. No patients, one other customer."

"Spontaneously the owner starts talking to the other customer about patients. Answering a question of mine, he says: 'Yes, they come here. I know all of them. When you live with them you get to know them quickly.' He tells about a German who came to his bar to see patients but couldn't pick them out. The owner himself had already seen five patients pass by. The German finally pointed to someone who wasn't a patient at all."

" 'A lot of them come here on the weekend, but also sometimes during the week.' Pointing to another bar: 'That's the first and the final stop. Oh, we sometimes get one at midnight or at one o'clock. Those are the good patients. They are allowed somewhat more privileges by their host family. But everything has changed now. It used to be easier to recognize them. They all had special clothing then. There were more funny guys among them but lately they have become much choosier in the Kolonie. We serve them beer, but not too much. As a matter of fact they aren't allowed to have any, but if we don't give them too much it won't harm them.' The owner's wife speaks: 'When I see one getting drunk and he asks for more beer, then I say: 'Jeff, you'll have to drink something else.' They're not always happy with that, but if they can't take it, they'd better go somewhere else. We don't want any trouble with them.' "

"Next, the owner and his wife start telling stories about patients they have known. Wife: 'You wouldn't believe it, but there are some very smart guys among the patients. One of them is N. He regularly went to the P. (another bar). You could ask him anything you wanted, he would always give you an answer. Also any date of birth or date of death of any prince or king. Or if you gave him your date of birth he would say what day of the week it was and what kind of weather around that time of the year. But you had to pay him for it. He wouldn't say anything without being paid. He could sit there and stare at a particular point for half an hour. It could be your nose or a chair. He could also look at you with penetrating eyes. I never felt at ease when he was looking at me like that.' "

"Owner: 'There was also a doctor (the wife knew him very well). You weren't allowed in his room and he kept receiving letters addressed to his doctor's title and also drug samples. He cured one of the children of the family. But he never came to the bar.' "

"The wife talks about another patient: 'O very often visited us and was very nice to our daughters. He received a large pension and wasn't allowed to spend all that money, so it was put in a bank for him. Because he had become a very good friend of ours, he wanted to leave the money to our daughters. Some time before he died he even tried to change his will to make that possible. But he couldn't do it because he was married. And though his wife hadn't paid him a single visit during the 30 years he was here, she arrived the day he died to collect his things. Isn't that cruel? She had never looked after him, but then she ran off with everything he had! If he had been able to give it to our daughters, we could have set up something for them with the money. It had to be a considerable amount, because a couple of weeks before his death he told me he had 400,000 francs ($10,000) in the bank alone. The people of the Kolonie must also have felt uneasy after such an affair. Of course they also hoped to get his property.' "

" 'He was a very good man. One time he said he intended to buy a bicycle for our oldest daughter. I told him: 'No, you can't give something to the one and nothing to the other. If you give something to one of them, you should give something to the other one, too! So he bought two bicycles. Another time he saw some Smyrna carpets made at the Rijkskolonie and he wanted to buy me one. I said: 'OK' He brought it here and he asked me if I liked it. I said if he had chosen it for me, it was OK with me and I would gladly accept it. I still have it upstairs.' "

"Owner about a 'difficult' patient: 'One time he came here late in the evening. There were a lot of people in the bar. Suddenly he was involved in a fight. I intervened and took him by his collar without thinking that he could easily have given me a beating. 'Get out!', I yelled. It worked. Later he tried to come here again. But I yelled at him: 'Go home and don't let me see your face again!' Afterwards I realized I had been a little too hard to him because the poor guy had left his raincoat in the bar. The poor guy! He has been punished now. He has to stay in the Kolonie every week, for 150 weeks in a row!' (This punishment was not imposed solely for this incident.) Wife: 'Yes, they're all scared of my husband. Because he can give them such a dirty look. But you have to be able to manage them. Sometimes I am very happy my husband is back home because they're not so scared of me.' "

"Wife about a patient who had drunk too much: 'After his third glass he started to act funny. He could only walk backwards. Right away I let him into the kitchen and gave him some strong coffee to drink. He emptied the whole pot but I didn't make him pay. It was better that nothing happened. Another one also could not hold his liquor. He had one beer and then collapsed. After a while he recovered and left the bar. Afterwards I heard that an ambulance picked him up a little bit later. He had a hole in his head and was kept in the hospital for two weeks.' "

"The owner about a patient who was a musician: 'He went everywhere with the band to play, and he was treated just like the other members. Of course, his friends bought him a lot of beer. People like him didn't have the money for all those things.' – 'Why aren't there any patients now who are members of the band?' – 'There don't seem to be any men with such talent anymore at the Kolonie. Centuries ago, the founder of the band was a patient.' "

"Saturday evening, January 1, 7:45. A single patient, a regular customer. Standing at the bar, drinking with a few customers. The same evening between 8:45 and 11:45. No patients; only a group of boisterous men."

"Sunday afternoon, January 2, between 4 and 5. Present: eight patients, three customers, the owner's wife, and another lady. All the patients are sitting at the bar. All but one are drinking beer, and he's drinking coffee from a big mug. During the one hour we were there, they all drank four glasses of beer; even the one drinking coffee was urged by the wife to have another one. It all happens in a friendly and personal tone: 'Come on, N, drink some more.' Two patients buy us a beer. The atmosphere is very friendly, companiable. The owner's wife says: 'They all come from you know where.' And when patient N starts chatting, she says: 'If you don't leave and sit in another chair he'll keep you busy until tomorrow morning!' About another patient: 'That's a good one!' A patient enters, receives a few francs from the woman and leaves. He is making the rounds for New Year's. The owner's wife gives me a signal each time a patient who is talking with me or with someone else says something that may be funny."

Case 6

A report filed by another team member at a later date describes a situation where patients are treated impersonally and where it is possible to speak of exploitation.

"Sunday afternoon, February 23, 1975 between 3:30 and 5. A popular bar. A big crowd is present. All chairs are taken and about 10 patients are standing at the bar. Most customers seem to be patients. There are also a few Italian immigrants. Two waitresses, wearing a kind of imitation Spanish dress. Most of the patients are silent and look around. Cheap songs urge the customers to dance. There are no songs juᶜt for listening in the jukebox. The waitresses are available for 'intimate' dancing. One couple is flirting on a bench. The atmosphere is very loose. A conversation between two patients: 'With these women you can't do anything anyway, because they always get injections. . . .' Discussion on the theme: 'Is it every month or every two weeks?' Alcohol consumption is very high and a lot of money is being spent. Someone buys a round for a table. One of the patients refuses because his glass is still half full. The one who is buying insists. One of the waitresses puts the glass of the man who has refused to his mouth and holds it there until he has finished. The one who is buying says: 'Now, this is a place where you're well looked after, isn't that right?' "

"I order mineral water and suspect I have received a glass of ordinary tapwater. Afterwards I order a glass of lemonade and receive a glass of clear liquid that seems to be water. When I draw the waitress' attention to the fact that I had ordered lemonade, she answers: 'I thought you ordered mineral water!' I think she thought I was a new patient-customer, because when I leave she says: 'Have a good afternoon and till next Sunday!' "

The preceding cases, given in detail because of their vividness, allow an analysis of the relational patterns that have developed in and around the Geel bars between patients and other people.

Based on the available data, we can say that a clear line is drawn by the participants between 'the people of the Kolonie' and the others. Patients never participate as peers, as belonging to the same class as the other customers, not even in the bars where the owners and the public are very tolerant towards them and where they are regularly involved in the company's conversations and actions. This 'line' between patients and 'normal' people is maintained in different ways.

In some bars, the people from the Kolonie are excluded as much as possible. A physical-spatial barrier is drawn and an attempt is made to prevent contact between patients and 'normals.' This appears to be the case in four types of bars: (1) establishments exclusively or nearly exclusively frequented by 'better class' people; (2) most of the 'youth bars'-discotheques (3) brothels; and (4) 'intimate' bars, simulating a brothel-like image without actually being such. Only in types (3) and (4) are patients refused service. In other cases it is done more indirectly. The result, however, is the same. These four types are drinking establishments that deviate from the traditional rural pattern and are products and agents of urbanization and industrialization. Businesses geared to the 'upper' classes are only viable because enough industry has located in Geel and surroundings to create a clientele that regularly patronizes restaurants and hotels. The discotheques are a recent phenomenon booming everywhere in the Kempen and are associated with so-called modern times and the 'emancipation' of young people. One of the older priests of Geel, who has been active in youth affairs for more than 30 years, considers the youth bars to be one of the region's recent evils. It is clear that brothels and brothel-like bars do not fit into the traditional rural environment and can also be viewed as a product of urbanization.

In bars where patients are regular customers, the line between illness and health is drawn in a more subtle fashion and is of a different nature.

As far as we could ascertain, patients are always identified as patients in the presence of outsiders. Either bartenders and customers overtly or covertly mention that they are patients, doing this in such a way the patients do not notice, or they act and talk to them in a manner that clearly indicates what kind of persons they are talking to. When interaction takes place, it is immediately signaled who is who.

When engaging in a conversation with patients, the tone is either jocular or benevolent and condescending. The condescending tone signals that one is speaking with an inferior. The joking tone suggests that the person spoken to is not accepted as a full-fledged conversational partner. At the same time the jocular tone signifies that the content of the conversation should not be taken seriously. It is a dialogue where 'funny' passages may occur and no one need think that the 'normal' partner is being duped. In certain cases the conversation is manipulated so that the patient's 'craziness' is exhibited before all. The conversation will turn to the patient's 'visions' or his 'big money,' and so on. A drunk customer will even exclaim—contrary to Geel tradition—: "You are a patient!"

Occasionally verbal ridicule of the patient escalates to sexual provocation, with full knowledge that nothing like a relationship can follow and that a call to the Rijkskolonie is sufficient to make the patient harmless in the event he ever becomes aggressive.

Provoking patients a little on the dance floor seems to be tolerated without evoking any reaction from the public. He can be laughed at to his face, he can be refused several dances in a humiliating manner, all without provoking any social response. Everyone accepts that one relates to patients in a different way than to ordinary human beings. The patient's social inferiority is taken for granted, because he is one from 'under the high trees'—a euphemism for the psychiatric hospital. (The road running alongside the hospital used to be lined with tall trees.)

The jocular tone, the content of the conversation, as well as the liberties taken in various situations can be interpreted as expressions of a joking relationship reflecting the following

social identity and social roles. Normal Geelians accept meeting patients in their leisure time at bars. They are willing to
talk to them and to relate to them and even to dance with
them; they also accept the patients' deviant language and
behavior. On the other hand, they expect everyone to agree
that in such situations they will not act seriously. The normal
customer feels that he belongs in a qualitatively different
category than his sick counterpart and expresses this in his
symmetrical joking relationship: the patient may tell all kinds
of strange and incoherent stories (he mostly does this uncon-
sciously) but the latter may reply in a like manner (consciously) without offending any bystanders. The 'normal'
partner, however, has to respect certain limits: he may not
really anger the patient nor may he repeatedly and con-
temptuously tell him he is crazy.

From the above it is clear that a definite line is drawn
between patients and healthy people in bars. Except for
places from which patients are barred, this line does not take
the form of spatial discrimination. Rather, it is expressed in
the kind of language used and in the liberties taken in
behavior towards patients. This line is not permanently maintained. Usually it is indicated at intervals. The deviant
language and behavior of patients lend continuity to the
duality, normal-mentally ill. In other words, in a bar situation
a patient is never continually treated as if he were healthy.
Socially he is kept in 'his place.' Interpretation of the *psychological* meaning of this for the patients is outside our competence.

In spite of this line between normal persons and mental
patients, patients have the opportunity to interact with
healthy persons within different contexts.

A patient may gossip in bars, malign his host family,
establish a friendship with the owner, the personnel, or other
customers. He may come into contact with people from
other families and bring diversification to his relationships.
He may play pool, observe, and even dance. If he wants to,

he may, at least verbally, joke with members of the opposite sex about sexual matters. Sometimes this may lead to a caricature of a sexual relationship. His erotic desires can be satisfied somewhat or fanned by dancing with normal girls and women or with patients of the opposite sex. In a lot of bars he may get slightly drunk, especially if the owners know that he can take it. Some patients can indulge their alcoholism. A certain amount of voyeurism is not denied to certain patients in youth bars. A patient may engage in conversation and become totally involved, even though his 'normal' listeners do not take him seriously. A limited number of patients find in the bars they regularly patronize a second, third, or fourth home, where they spend part of day and evening as customers with certain acquired rights.

All this happens in an atmosphere that allows the patients to feel free: they are not directly controlled or protected. The few restrictions imposed on them to prevent objections and trouble with the Rijkskolonie are of an indirect nature.

Every patient knows at what time he must be home, which is determined by the district nurse after consultation with the host family. Some host families are very strict in this regard, others are more lenient. The 'best' patients can officially stay out until midnight on weekends.

Furthermore, patients probably do not feel restricted by the fact that they are not welcome in certain establishments. Socially, they do not feel at home there, and enough places exist where, in their own fashion, they can be part of the crowd.

In bars they are not obliged to sit in a particular corner; they can sit wherever they want. The prohibition against selling beer to patients, decreed by the Rijkskononie, is nowhere heeded, except when the bartender hears that the consumption of alcohol will result in trouble. The refusal to sell beer is used as a means to keep patients out.

Patients are not especially protected from the other customers. Discussions in bars range over all kinds of events and subjects, except mental illness itself, insofar as it could relate directly to the patient. Patients risk, more than other customers, being teased, mostly in a good-natured way, but sometimes it may become cruel. Patients are not spared because they are patients. Geelians have always known patients and probably always will and nobody thinks of imposing special restrictions either on themselves or on others because of their presence.

When other people offer patients a whole range of interaction possibilities in the framework of bars, they do it spontaneously and without conscious therapeutic goals. No situation nor interview reflected any therapeutic concern. Patients are a special kind of people, but they are people, and they are customers. If they have money, they are not to be sent away.

Here the question of abuses can be raised.

Members of the nursing staff have pointed out that some bartenders are suspected of urging patients to drink. Our observations seem to confirm this. Moreover, it is likely that patients are cheated in some drinking establishments and that they do not get real value for their money. As far as we could ascertain, these abuses never seem to be great and only occur in a limited number of bars. It is possible, however, that some patients drink more than is healthy. Several patients were observed by our researcher in a semidrunk state and one bartender said that one patient drinks as many as 14 large glasses of beer in one evening. We cannot say if some patients undermine their health by drinking, thus decreasing their chances for mental recovery. The Rijkskolonie seems to have answered this question by prohibiting the serving of alcoholic beverages to patients and by refusing, in recent years, to board patients with bar owners.

No single observation, direct or indirect, nor any interview, gave us reason to suspect that some drinking establishments offered patients the opportunity to carry on sexual activities that might have severe social consequences. As far as we know, Geel bars do not offer sanctuaries for illicit relationships or adventures involving patients. A well known brothel, now closed, absolutely refused admittance to patients. Another brothel follows the same policy. The managers are well aware that breaching this code would have far-reaching consequences, both legal and social. On the other hand, we know with certainty that some patients visit brothels. But they do this in towns where they are not known. Sexual affairs in Geel involving patients usually occur in the woods and in the isolated countryside.

Therapists may wonder, when reading these data, to what extent the erotic possibilities offered to patients are favorable to their mental health. Erotic contact with the other sex is generally allowed in a humiliating context, without there ever being an opportunity for sexual relations. However, we can hardly find fault with the bartenders for this. The fact that patients have the opportunity for erotic activities is a direct consequence of the fact that they are allowed to participate in, and are integrated into, the local community. Waitresses and bartender's wives who try to appear as sexy as possible do not do this primarily to attract patients, but to attract customers in general.

At present there are no bars where strangers can come to look at patients, and we do not know if they ever existed. Businesses using this kind of 'attraction' as publicity were not found. It is true, however, that some bartenders are inclined to use patients to amuse their other customers. But actual exploitation in this respect does not seem to occur.

Finally, we may ask to what extent patients interfere with bar life in Geel.[2] Can a 'normal' Geelian who does not want to be involved in family care go and have a beer without having to be in the presence of patients? Yes. Out of 106 bar visits lasting an average of 45 minutes, our researcher met one or more patients only 33 times. In total he observed only 57 patients. Except for a few cases of regular customers described above, patients' visits remain confined to the afternoons and evenings of Saturdays and Sundays and the days of the local fair. The large majority of patients follow the rural norm, and consider going to bars during the week as unusual and a waste of money.

NOTES

1. 'Joking relationship' is a technical anthropological term that is defined by A. R. Radcliffe-Brown as follows: "What is meant by the term 'joking relationship' is a relation between two persons in which one is by custom permitted, and in some instances required, to tease or make fun of the other, who in his turn is required to take no offense. It is important to distinguish two main varieties. In one the relation is symmetrical; each of the two persons teases or makes fun of the other. In the other variety the relation is asymmetrical." (*Structure and Function in Primitive Society,* London, Cohen and West, 1963, pp. 90-91.) And also: "The joking relationship is a peculiar combination of friendliness and antagonism. The behavior is such that in any other special context it would express and arouse hostility; but it is not meant seriously and must not be taken seriously. There is a pretence of hostility and real friendliness." (Ibidem, p. 91.)

2. On the Geelians' attitude towards boarder participation in community life, see G. Hedebouw, *Houding ten aanzien van Geel en de Geelse Gezinsverpleging,* pp. 114-118.

A rural corner of Geel.

Chapter 8

BOARDERS AND THE VOLUNTARY ASSOCIATIONS

The network of the social relationships in Geel extends beyond the immediate Geel region. Many Geelians work outside Geel, go for rides by car, or spend their holidays somewhere else. Some have regional as well as national and international business contacts[1]. By radio, and more so by television, Geel comes into contact with the world scene. Therefore, Geel cannot be considered as a closed rural community. The voluntary associations, of which many Geelians are members, mainly limit their activities to the Geel territory. There is a wide range of such associations. We were able to find as many as 87 Catholic associations in addition to a large number of associations of various political and philosophical tendencies[2].

The groups under investigation (the 87 Catholic associations) can be divided into three main categories:

(1) Organizations whose activities mainly, if not exclusively, take place within the church building. We call them in-church organizations.

(2) Traditional associations of the extra-church type. Though Catholic, they are not directly involved with the liturgy. These associations are in most cases affiliated to regional or national groups. This category can be further divided into: professional associations, cultural and recreational associations, and youth movements, with mainly an educational role and which offer leisure time activities to youngsters.

(3) Recent renewal groups, created after Vatican II and reflecting a change in the mentality and structure of the Church and of society.

This classification is rather rudimentary: our aim here is not to explain the structures and the functioning of Geel organizations, but only to examine which relationships have developed between these social entities and the Rijkskolonie patients.

All Geel parishes had, until some 10 years ago, a number of religious associations whose main objective was to stimulate the faithful to regular ritual and devotional practice. One of these groups was the *Bond van het Heilig Hart* (Association of the Sacred Heart) which had a large number of members, both national and international, and was divided into male and female sections. The collective activity of the members included monthly participation in Holy Mass and Communion. In order to facilitate control over this religious practice, every member had to hand in an attendance card when entering the church. The association had smaller groups, the 'devotees', who, per district, supervised the other members and if necessary encouraged them to more regularity. These devotees were also charged with the recruitment of new members.

The Association of the Sacred Heart is practically the only association—besides some other less important in-church associations—that gave full membership to large numbers of patients. It is difficult to state the exact number, but it certainly was a double-digit figure. The social implications of membership for the patients were practically nonexistent. It simply implied the passive presence of the boarders at the monthly mass of the association. Without being a member they could attend mass as well because the masses were open to everyone. As for all other liturgical rites, the boarders were simply requested not to disturb them. As always under similar circumstances, those patients whose behavior was too distracting were kept at home by the host families.

The attribution of memberships to Rijkskolonie patients did not at all imply that priests or other members thought the patients capable of understanding the meaning or the association's activities, and it certainly did not mean that they considered the patients as adult moral personalities. The attitude of the ecclesiastical authorities and of all the host families (we have interviewed all of them concerning this) can be summarized as follows: the Rijkskolonie patients are not subject to the moral and religious rules that normally apply to healthy Catholics. "There is a reason for their being here!" There is something wrong with each of them and, therefore, they are not normal persons who can be considered religiously and morally responsible. The interviews with priests clearly showed that patients, in pastoral matters, were almost exclusively referred to the jurisdiction of the chaplain of the Rijkskolonie. No other priests ever thought of taking initiatives in this area, which, strictly speaking, does not belong to his jurisdiction. The sick people have their own priest. Thus, this moral and religious separation of the boarders, which dates back to an episcopal decision of the second half of the nineteenth century,[3] has a legal basis, having been officially recognized and sanctioned.

This basic attitude, that all Rijkskolonie patients are morally and religiously infants unless the contrary is proven, is reflected in the attitudes of the local priests and the ecclesiastical hierarchy. None of the present parish priests can remember any measures ever taken by the diocese concerning the patients of the Rijkskolonie. All responsibility for them was left to the chaplain of the Rijkskolonie. Although the hierarchy has always been very much concerned with 'dignified' Communion, and although divorced and remarried people were refused Communion, the Last Sacraments, and an ecclesiastical funeral (obstinate sinners were in some cases refused forgiveness, and so on), no such measures were ever taken towards the Rijkskolonie patients. As far as we could determine, the Geel parish priests have always defended the view that patients should be allowed to participate in accordance with their capabilities. Only very disturbing elements were kept out of church. Thus, patients were allowed Confession and if they wished, went to Communion. This was seen as being entirely in accord with traditional ecclesiastical practice: patients are not totally, and very often not at all, responsible and therefore no sin can be committed. Even if they go to the Communion in an objectively unworthy condition one cannot speak of serious guilt. Therefore, the priests did not feel they were accessories. Moreover, one never knows when and to what extent patients have lucid moments, so that it would be wrong to prevent their participation in religious practice. In this context, boarders are considered as 'poor' who cannot be expelled from the company of the faithful unless they obstruct collective rites by extremely deviant behavior.

The fact that patients are accepted as full members of pious organizations is then only a logical consequence. The social inconveniences resulting from this situation for other members were minimal or even nonexistent, and everyone was aware that boarders were only accepted 'in accordance with their capabilities.' Such membership did not degrade the other members and did not influence any personal interaction. There was only a collective relationship to God, about which only the parish priest spoke during his sermon.

Nowhere, however, did we find any trace of a patient having been a 'devotee.' We do not mean to suggest that this was, psychologically or socially, possible, thereby accusing the ecclesiastical hierarchy of discrimination toward the patients. We only want to draw attention to the fact that in this association the patients played a passive role.

Most of these pious associations, in which patients had full membership, have completely or partially disappeared during the last 10 years due to liturgical and other changes in the Catholic church. Only in four of the 12 parishes of Geel do we find remnants of the Association of the Sacred Heart. These four parishes are situated on the outskirts of the town and serve the more rural areas of Geel. In the other parishes the association has disappeared. The faithful have looked for other means of expression. The same applies for the other pious movements.

But it has struck the chaplain of the Rijkskolonie during his annual pastoral visits, without his being able to produce exact figures, that a large number of patients were very upset about the disappearance of these associations. They attached much importance to their membership. Their anger also pertains to liturgical changes. Most of what the patients had learned is now outdated and they feel disoriented. A small minority is highly indignant and refuses to go to church any longer because Latin and the traditional liturgical forms have been abolished.

The 'normal' *active* Catholics in Geel, however, are exploring other possibilities. After the Second Vatican Council, a more active participation of laymen in the church was initiated. The meeting where only the parish priest speaks—thus giving the layman an almost completely passive role—has been abandoned. The 'active' faithful, who formerly would have assumed the role of 'devotees' in the Association of the Sacred Heart, are now involved in discussion groups or in other units taking a specific social concern as religious points of action. In all the Geel parishes, and especially in the four central ones, such 'new' associations have been founded. They discuss problems of faith, of marriage, and of youth, and regularly organize activities concerning handicapped people, developing countries, and the like. In these groups, whose members are willing to do something for a living church and their faith, emphasis is put on personal involvement and responsibility. Exchange, reciprocity, communication, and cooperation are therefore explicitly stressed. Thus, it is no wonder that the Rijkskolonie patients are given no chance whatsoever to participate in these groups, especially if we consider the idea that the 'people from the Kolonie' are not thought to be morally or religiously responsible. Indeed, nobody can deny that it is easier for the patients to participate passively in the Holy Mass than in the activities of these new groups. It is obvious that the latter trend was also made possible by the continuous increase in the number of educated people at Geel. Because there is longer and more intensive schooling, more and more people can take part in discussions, speak publicly, and run meetings, whereas before only the priests and the well educated thought themselves able to do so.

In the area of social and religious life, this form of modernization has enlarged the gap between 'normal' Geelians and the patients. In the past, patients could sit next to other members of the association during the celebration of Mass and outwardly act alike. Nowadays, boarders cannot enter the room or the private houses where the new religious meetings are held. Our investigation has shown that these groups have never thought of the Rijkskolonie patients as a possible aim for their charitable activities, although they concentrate explicitly on minorities and 'loners.' For example, they visit the sick and the lonely. On Christmas they went to the Rijkskolonie and gave presents to the nurses and orderlies who were on duty that particular holiday. They thought that these people would feel a bit lonely on this very special day, even if this was a result of their commitment to serve humanity. But apparently nobody thought of the patients, many of whom were certainly lonely that day also. This thought has never occurred to these Geelians, whose merits and honest social involvement can hardly be doubted.

In the more traditional associations, the theme of the boarder has never been considered either, although numerous humanitarian actions have been carried out. We do not intend to make any moral judgment. We simply want to draw attention to factual data caused by the very special position of the boarders in the Geel system.

Other facts also point to this particular position of the patients. All interviewed executive committee members were very surprised when the researcher, in this case the chaplain of the Rijkskolonie, asked them if they had ever thought of accepting patients as members of their associations. In most cases this immediately caused guilt feelings and most committees reacted by saying they would seriously consider the matter. We should stress that this was the overall and general reaction. Profound shame was expressed by the executive committee of an association dealing with the integration of the socially deprived and especially the handicapped into existing associations in Geel. This organization at one time had tried, but without success, to integrate into associations with those mentally handicapped who had been *born in Geel*, but nobody had ever associated this category of people with the boarders. One leader of a youth movement expressed his regret by comparing the social structure of Geel to an *apartheid* situation in which people are segregated and one group is strongly discriminated against.

When the persons interviewed had overcome their surprise caused by the question of boarders being members of their association, they started rationalizing about this state of affairs. A whole series of objections was raised against such membership. Because these objections were spontaneous utterances, they can be considered expressions of unconscious or semiconscious attitudes towards the patients. Below is a list of these objections (between parenthesis we have indicated the number of people in agreement with the opinion):

(1) The Rijkskolonie patients belong to a special category with specific behavior patterns. (three)

(2) The Kolonie also considers them a special group. The patients continue to be regarded as such. (three)

(3) Even if they are more intelligent than some other members, they still remain disturbed people. (two)

(4) They do not belong to the community, have any rights, because they have no identity cards. (one)

(5) You cannot take them seriously. They are marked. (three)

(6) It is improbable that we could realize the integration of patients, even in an association for handicapped persons, because even there the mentally handicapped are kept apart as much as possible. (one)

(7) We would devalue our organization in the eyes of the other members if we were to accept patients for membership, even if the patients could participate intelligently. (seven)

(8) We could get into trouble with the patients. (two)

(9) We must draw the line somewhere: who may be accepted and who may not. (one) (It would be difficult to allow some patients to join and not others.)

(10) Patients would create inappropriate disturbances. (one)

(11) Patients are not legally responsible. Can we then accept them as members? (one)

(12) With patients present we would not feel free anymore. (one)

(13) With patients present we would no longer feel that we were among our peers. (seven)

(14) The reason is not that they are disturbed or less intelligent; you find many people like that in many associations. But if those members were 'in the book' (registered Rijkskolonie patients) they would be rejected as well. (one)

(15) Tradition has considered the patients as inferior beings and 'outcasts.' Much has improved and patients seem to be less blunt. (one)

(16) Patients cannot pay membership fees. (six) However, much has been changed: patients can nowadays buy their own tobacco. In the past they used to collect cigarette butts. In bars they can pay for a glass of beer and are accepted in billiard and card games. (one)

(17) Many host families do not like their boarders to mix with other people from the same street or district, and they do not wish them to participate in associations (because the patients know too much about the host family). (one)

(18) Patients have no interest in becoming members. What could they possibly do? (nine)

(19) The association is aimed at a certain category of people (with specific interests) and the patients do not belong to any interest group. (eleven)

(20) Patients would be teased too much. (one)

(21) Patients would be criticized more than other members. (one)

(22) In serious matters less is tolerated of the patient. (one)

(23) Few patients would ever qualify as members. (Almost all executive committees.)

(24) The patients themselves do not wish to join. They prefer to stay outside. (one)

(25) Patients would not feel at home. They always stick together in sports and at leisure. (one)

(26) The Kolonie itself is a major obstacle. In the past it always kept patients separate, even by imposing a special uniform on the patients. (one)

(27) The Kolonie imposes all kinds of restrictions: patients have to be at home at a specific time and cannot go wherever they want. (fifteen)

(28) The Kolonie requires permission even to join the patients' own clubs, e.g., the sports club, or the Kolonie's club, or the 'Klimop.' Even going to school was forbidden in the past. (one)

(29) Anyway, the Kolonie takes care of everything the patients need. (one)

From the preceding list we can derive the following basic themes:

(1) The patients of the Rijkskolonie are considered as a very special class of people.

(2) They are marked and stigmatized.

(3) Even if they are as intelligent as 'normal' Geelians, this does not erase their stigma: 'they are in the book.'

(4) You cannot take the Rijkskolonie patients seriously in social life outside the family without making a fool of yourself.

(5) Almost no patients would qualify to become a member of an association.

(6) Patients would misbehave in an association.

(7) The Rijkskolonie does not seem to wish or to encourage the integration of patients into associations.

(8) The Rijkskolonie takes care of the patients' leisure time, and so on. Healthy Geelinas need not to do so.

Almost all executive committees would require that, were a patient to attend a meeting, he would have to be accompanied by a member of the host family. They are afraid that patients would try to draw attention to themselves or provoke incidents by disruptive behavior.

The fact that most executive committees have agreed in principle to accept patients on an experimental basis seems to prove that they are not very sure about the incapacity of the patients or, at least, that the systematic exclusion of boarders is a kind of odium that may burden their association.

The surprising effect of the interviewer's questions shows that, as far as the associations are concerned, the 'apartheid' of the patients is a cultural phenomenon of which the interviewed people have suddenly become aware. In their minds the patients had never been considered in terms of membership in free associations, except in very exceptional circumstances, as was the case of the patient who had been the band leader. There may be a few other exceptions, as we shall see further on, but in the present situation full membership for patients in 'serious' organizations is virtually excluded.

None of the interviewed committee members knew any ex-patients who were members of an association. Some cases were remembered: an ex-patient, a baker, might have been a member of the National Christian Association of the Self-Employed (NCMV). Another was a member of the Boerenbond (Farmers' Union), another a member of the Catholic Workers' Union (KWB), and a female ex-patient a member of the Catholic Women Workers (KAV).

Although the integration of patients has never been the subject of meetings, some sporadic efforts have been made to accept patients in associations. In one single instance, the

Young Catholic Workers (KAJ) tried to accept a patient, but this venture failed when the patient was transferred. Alcoholics Anonymous made another such attempt, but the patient did not obtain permission from the Rijkskolonie. Two other attempts to accept people in a church choir failed because of administrative complications. One association has accepted a patient as a member, but nobody within the association except the executive committee, *not even the patient himself,* knows that he is being supervised by the Rijkskolonie. Some patients are members of a model club where they pay 10 francs membership dues. In a Catholic association of retired people, one patient was a member, but there was some trouble with him, so they had to ask him to leave. The local section of the Catholic Rural Youth (KLJ) had a female patient as a member, but she was transferred. Sometimes one finds a patient as a member of a band, a soccer team, or a gymnastics club.

These facts show that in spite of a separation between Geelians and patients in most of the associations, this situation cannot be described as apartheid. Occasional attempts are made to accept patients as members, and the physical presence of patients is not repulsed. The latter is confirmed by the participation of a number of patients, as nonmembers, in the activities of associations. In 34 of the 87 associations under investigation, a small number of patients occasionally take part in a subordinate role. In 12 of these 34 associations, the patient is accompanied by a member of the host family. These 12 cases are related to associations for adults. In youth movements, the patients were not accompanied.

There are at most four patients in the same organization as participants in some activity. Five patients participate in fishing; seven participate in sports; seven in gymnastic events; three do some manual labor in an association; six of them go for trips with the association; and six participate in fairs or dances. Altogether there are more or less 50 patients involved in leisure activities of associations. On the other hand, boarders are never present in training courses or other 'serious' activities.

Various sociocultural factors may explain the above-described situation.

Most associations came into existence in the course of this century. Compared to the patient care system, they have a very short history. Their foundation is related to the development of interest groups in the Geel community, which gradually developed and whose population gradually differentiated into different socioeconomic groups.

Almost all the local associations are branches of national or regional associations. Therefore, their statutes, objectives, and activities are mostly determined from the outside. Obviously, such associations, and especially pressure groups defending socioeconomic interests, provide no possibilities for the mentally handicapped. The training of staff members, programs, slogans, and activities, all of which are launched on a national level, obviously do not take into account the presence of boarders in Geel. This is one reason why boarders are not accepted in these associations. However, this still does not fully explain the situation because most associations regularly focus on specific actions in the local community. They help the ill, collect money for handicapped children, visit lonely people in the area, and so on. Why then are the 'people of the Rijkskolonie' excluded from all this as far as membership is concerned, as well as from humanitarian actions that could be carried out in their behalf?

Many committee members have stated that boarders in Geel belong to a special social category, even if they board with Geel families and walk in the streets and go to the bars. In the past patients were socially distinguished by their compulsory uniforms. Everybody could then recognize and distinguish patients from other people. Since the uniform was abolished the distinction had become somewhat vague but still continues to exist. The main criterion now for belonging to this special category of people is not only being disturbed but being 'in the book' or belonging to the Rijkskolonie. The disturbed and the mentally handicapped who are born in Geel are almost never entrusted to the Rijkskolonie. They belong to another category. Thus, we can explain why the Geel association dealing especially with handicapped people, including the mentally handicapped, has never considered the boarders, though it is obvious that everybody belonging to the Rijkskolonie can be considered to have a mental handicap.

As far as public social life is concerned, the boarders are primarily the responsibility of the Rijkskolonie. Therefore, the Kolonie is first of all responsible for the organization of the patients' leisure time, which is taken care of quite adequately by organizing trips, fishing contests, and other sports activities. The Rijkskolonie also has a club, the *Klimop van de Kolonie* where patients can meet for party games. Moreover, the Rijkskolonie remains, for all Geelians and patients, an official institution which supervises the patients and with which all conflicts are best avoided. Patients are associated with the Rijkskolonie, and Geelians see the Rijkskolonie as a possible interfering authority behind every patient. Associations cannot grant official membership to a patient without previous permission by the Rijkskolonie. By formal contacts with the patient one automatically becomes involved with the official supervising authorities, and this certainly does not appeal to everybody. Thus, patients are in the most literal sense 'people of the Rijkskolonie.' They belong to it. They are supervised by it and the Rijkskolonie intervenes when things go wrong with the patients. The Rijkskolonie withdraws patients from unsuitable families, prohibits alcoholic beverages from being offered to patients, and determines the time when the patients must be in. This supervision by the Rijkskolonie, although very flexible and human, does not lend itself to the best of relationships with the population.

There seems to be another, much more fundamental reason why more efforts are not made to integrate patients

into associations dealing with serious matters. Their integration would mean abandoning the distinction between illness
and health—a distinction that has always been maintained in
the patient care system. Voluntary associations create the
possibility of engaging freely in a relationship with others on
a basis of equality. Every association thus sets conditions
guaranteeing the equality of its members. By accepting
Rijkskolonie patients those fundamental principles would be
abandoned. This explains the following reactions of the
executive committee members when asked about accepting
patients as members: "You cannot take the patients seriously." "We would devalue the associations in the opinion of
other members if we did so, even if the patients were mentally fit." "By accepting patients we would no longer be
amongst our peers." "Our association is aimed at a specific
category of people, and the boarders do not belong to any
category." And so on.

As we shall show in another chapter, the distinction
between ill and healthy people is understandable given, as we
know, that the majority of the patients are what medical
psychiatry considers 'chronic cases.' These patients have
almost no chance of recovery. This, however, does not mean
that no patients could be reintegrated into normal life. There
are such patients, though their numbers are small, who are
being denied the chance to function again in a larger community.

As far as public social life is concerned, patients have not
only their 'time,' but also their 'place.'

We want to stress this present situation because many false
ideas about the Geel community have arisen from superficial
descriptions and idealistic writings. Furthermore, we thought
it necessary to describe which conscious and unconscious
techniques are used in Geel in order to live and continue to
live with seriously mentally handicapped people. We do not
want to suggest that associations should take patients as
members nor that they should organize help for the patients.

One can only carefully experiment so the balance of the whole system would not be disturbed.

Nevertheless, we think it possible that, for therapeutic objectives, a collaboration between the Rijkskolonie and various associations could lead to the integration of some patients as full members. This also appears from the answers of the various executive committee members. We are convinced that if such a form of patient integration was proposed to those committees, they would cooperate. Handling the problem in this way indeed means that the basic distinction between patients and other members is maintained as in the host families. Thus, the 'normal' member would act as a sort of hidden therapeutist and not as structurally equivalent to the patient. On the other hand, we are not convinced that this new role of the associations would destroy the therapeutic effect of 'total integration' because this kind of integration would not be genuinely total. In this way a certain category of patients, who are capable of improvement and further socialization, would be given new possibilities to gradually and more autonomously adapt to the 'outside world.'

NOTES

1. See: J. DUPRE, Economische Ontwikkeling en Industrialisatie, and A. PALS-GHOOS, Maatschappelijke Verschijnselen tijdens Industriële Expansie, In: Geel, Geel, Lions Geel-Mol, 1976, pp. 288-307 and pp. 311-314.

2. See the list given by W. DE SMET in his article "Sociaal-cultureel Verenigingsleven" in Geel, pp. 399-401. We thought it unnecessary to investigate these associations further because our research concerning the patients' social network had shown that almost no patients were members of these associations.

3. K. VERAGHTERT, unpublished paper.

An attempt at a modern shopping center.

Chapter 9

INTIMATE RELATIONSHIPS

In Geel, all boarders live in more or less compulsory celibacy. Obviously, this situation entails problems. Nevertheless, nothing remarkable was observed in Geel in this respect. On the contrary, although almost all patients reside with families where there are persons of the opposite sex, and many boarders are allowed to walk freely in the community, the number of incidents occasioned by them is so low that we cannot speak of any sexual criminality.

The patients' sexual life, like the entire field of private sexuality, is a sensitive matter about which very little is spoken in Geel. It seemed unwarranted to discuss these problems with the patients themselves. In some interviews patients troubled by sexual deviations were given the opportunity to speak about their problems. They did not take this opportunity. Moreover, it seemed probable that we would have caused much turmoil in many boarders if we would have tried to discuss this topic systematically. Therefore, we investigated this matter indirectly. We asked for, and obtained, the cooperation of the host families. All host families were interviewed on this subject. Out of respect for the patients' privacy we will discuss this subject very concisely and only in general terms.

Among host families, 224 mentioned that their boarders (16.43% of the boarder population) had some kind of sexual problem. Only in a few sporadic cases had these problems given rise to serious confrontations between the patients and their environment. Generally speaking, the Geel system seems to keep the patients' sexuality under control and in the last decades Geel has in no way proved to be a dangerous town.

As long as the patients do not try to involve other persons in their sexuality, they are left alone. Traces found by the host families during domestic chores or direct observation have shown that many male patients (82) masturbate. Most host families feel these practices to be normal and never allude to them in front of the patients. Some host families remarked that boarders are people too and, as everyone else, should be allowed to have some satisfaction in their lives. Only a few host families notified the district nurses who then provided medication to suppress the patients' sexual inclinations. The only complaints some host families had concerning these masturbation practices was that they had some trouble keeping their patients' sheets and laundry clean.

The fact that most host families are traditional Catholics does not seem to result in their wanting to impose the sexual morality of the Catholic church. In so far as moral appraisals were formulated by host families, which was rarely the case, this was always done with tolerant understanding: "They are people too." What the patient does on his own in the privacy of his room is considered to be his business, and there is very rarely a reaction to it. On the other hand, the boarder is immediately reprimanded if he manifests himself sexually in the presence of family members or visitors. Masturbation in the presence of others is forbidden.

The same applies to exhibitionism. Thirteen such cases were reported. The patient is then told to go to his room immediately and get dressed. One of the host families made a 'compromise' with the boarder: he is allowed to sit naked in his room as long as he wants. In none of the reported cases was the patient's exhibitionism considered a serious matter. One incident showed it is against the Geel custom to react too strongly to such deviations. Once the daughter of a host family was alone in the house with the male patient. Suddenly the man appeared naked. The girl panicked and obtained help from the neighbors. The Rijkskolonie intervened and removed the patient from the family. The girl told one of our team members that she was very sorry that her uncontrolled reaction caused the patient to be removed from the family of which he had become a member. Indeed, such reactions are considered as undesirable and uncommon by the host families. The rule of thumb is never to show any fear of a boarder, and most cases can be resolved without the intervention of the Rijkskolonie. Deviant behavior should be dealt with in a quiet but assertive manner.

Another host family told us that several times their young and attractive patient appeared naked in front of the father when she was alone with him and had tried to seduce him. The young host couple, who had four children, decided they had to keep the patient because she would probably go astray again. As a child she had lived in several institutions and had already been removed or sent away from four other families.

Still other host families are very tolerant towards their patient's sexual deviations. Patient X, for example, is a fetishist. This young man regularly goes to the dump to collect women's underwear: girdles, panties, stockings, and bras. He keeps these things under his bed or under his mattress and uses them regularly while masturbating. He also takes women's underwear from the clothesline at the host family home and, afterwards, hangs them back up soiled. Despite attempts at correction, the patient cannot be dissuaded from his habits. So the host family contents itself with taking the boarder's unhygienic collection from his room and burning it now and then. It has been this way for years. The host family does not even consider sending the patient back to the Kolonie.

A restricted number of male patients regularly attempt to seek physical contact with the wife of the family, for example, by suddenly pressing his body against hers. Such actions are discouraged but never dramatized. The same is true for voyeurism.

Although host families consider it normal to take the patient's sexual deviations or undesirable manifestations quietly, severe action is taken against those patients showing pedophiliac tendencies. Such patients are never left alone with children. An equally severe attitude is taken towards any relationship that might lead to sexual intercourse. Regular visits by boarders to other patients or outsiders of the opposite sex are immediately reported to the host family or to the Rijkskolonie authorities. As is apparent from our study of Geel bar life, some patients are tolerated at dances where they may even joke about sexual matters, but it is inconceivable that pairing would be tolerated. It caused a stir in host family circles when, in 1974, one of the Rijkskolonie authorities gave certain patients written permission to visit (on Sundays) a patient of the opposite sex and go for a walk. This experiment was considered risky and dangerous, one that could lead to undesirable situations. Sexual relations between patients, who can never have a family, are disapproved of and forbidden by the Geel community, even though all fertile female patients are protected by contraceptives against the risks of unwanted pregnancies.

There are known cases of patient couples who, usually in the woods, were caught in the act of sexual intercourse. Of some patients we know with certainty that they occasionally go to brothels outside Geel. But these are exceptions. The system keeps a close and efficient watch on any sexual act involving other persons.

From the interviews we had in Geel with the parish priests and from reported cases and incidents, it appears that patients are not considered morally responsible for their sexual behavior. Confessors never question patients in the confessional about this domain, and if patients themselves mention facts related to this field, as little attention as possible is given to them. Host families do not link the patients' sexual behavior to Catholic morality nor to religion. The Catholic hierarchy, as far as we have been able to determine, has never addressed itself to these matters, not even when it was highly concerned with sexuality and the sexual life of the faithful. According to all principles of traditional, official ethics, patients fall in the category of people who are not, or not fully, responsible for their actions. No one in charge of them should worry about their salvation, even if outwardly they seem sinful as regards sexuality. Only when the patient's sexuality has social implications is some action taken. So in this domain, another aspect of the dichotomy between 'normals' and 'abnormals' is observed. All patients regardless of their individual status and possibilities are placed in one and the same category.

These data concerning the patients' sexual lives allow the following conclusions. A considerable number of patients clearly manifest sexual desires, which they can only satisfy by masturbating or seeking impersonal eroticism in certain bars or discotheques. Pairing is not allowed and sexual liaisons are inconceivable. The host families, and other persons involved in patient care for many years, fear that they would lose control over the patients if they allowed such things to happen, not to speak of the 'moral' implications for those who let them happen. The patients cannot be offered any opportunity for an adult sexual life.

Chapter 10

NORMAL AND ABNORMAL

So far, our study of the Geel home care system has dealt with several anthropological problems, such as the relationships between majority and minority groups, the status of 'normal' and 'abnormal' in a given cultural field, and social network and formal social structures.

We would now like to discuss further a number of these important problems.

The first problem that we shall treat concerns the relationship between majority and minority groups and the borderline separating these entities. How does the mechanism of social distinction function not only as far as attitudes and structural and conceptual aspects are concerned, but also on the level of actual interaction?

This theoretical problem coincides to some degree with the anthropological problem of the borderline between 'normal' and 'abnormal' in a cultural environment in which for centuries the 'sane' and the 'insane' have lived together.

When investigating the Geel situation these questions cannot be considered separately. The researchers continually experience and observe—independently of their theoretical point of view—forms of interaction between a majority of mentally healthy people and a minority composed exclusively of the mentally handicapped.

In discussing the status of 'normal' and 'abnormal' and the borderline separating them, one has to consider the extent to which the majority influences and conditions the minority's state of being. Some 'humanitarian' theories in psychiatry start from the assumption that the mentally handicapped person is first and foremost a human being whose social relationships are deranged, i.e., whose social being is deranged[1]. The patients' chances of self-realization in relationships with other people are of utmost importance to their recovery or improvement. From this point of view, the relationships developing between the boarders and the Geel residents are very important.

The traditional view of psychiatric institutions has been that confinement and supervision of the mentally ill are necessary for the protection of the healthy. This places the relationships between the mentally ill and the healthy of Geel in a somewhat different light, but it does not detract from the question. Thus, we can ask: Is the Geel system a safe place for the healthy community? How do healthy people keep the patients calm and harmless? What patterns have developed between the 'minority' and the 'majority' to maintain this calm?

When studying the relationships between the 'minority' and the 'majority,' we must first deal with the nature of 'mental illness' or 'mental handicap' because the Geelians are confronted with it as an inevitable part of their social life. Whether one considers 'mental illness' and 'feeblemindedness' primarily as products of society or chiefly as biological matters does not affect the fact that the patients at Geel are mentally disturbed, no matter how this disturbance is defined.

According to the Rijkskolonie, two-thirds of the patients are oligophrenics and one-third psychotics. No matter what the genesis or the cause of the present deficiencies may be, they exist and are apparent to everyone, either immediately or after a short period of time. In Belgian psychiatry Geel is known as a place where serious 'chronic' cases are sent. These cases offer little hope for recovery. Hence, Geelians rarely meet patients who suffer from incipient or very slight mental disturbances; they do not have the opportunity to experience 'mental health' and 'mental illness' as two extreme positions on a *continuum*. Most of the time they are confronted with chronic cases: the seriously deranged or infantile. This 'different way of being' manifests itself as deviant behavior.

In our analysis of the Geel 'folk theory' of the abnormal, let us start from the cases described in Chapter 2, and, in particular, the case of 'God' or the 'King,' one of the most popular and most spectacular cases in Geel. Many Geelians knew him and the fact that he identified with the Son of God was quite striking.

On the basis of his observable behavior, we may conclude that P, in his verbal accounts of his identity, his relationship to the world, to God, and to other people, totally deviates from the socioculture of the normal Geelians and from their way of perceiving him. He allots himself a double identity: He has two mothers, two fathers and, moreover, lives during the day on earth and at night in heaven. He is, at the same time, God and somebody whose identity papers are no longer valid. He is the Son of God and father of three children, of whom one regularly comes to visit him. He had also been married.

Nevertheless, not all of his observable behavior is deviant. When we arrived at the host family's house he was carefully sweeping the sidewalk and we would not have suspected he was a patient. He had also worked with the host family. But it is obvious that a large part of his behavior radically differs from what is acceptable for normal human beings. Nobody can accept P's identity as God or whatever is connected with this identity in the patient's account. The Geelians do not recognize P as God's son, and neither does the pastor or the pope, who does not even know P exists. It is clear to everyone that P neither goes to Antwerp every night nor does he go to heaven. It is also clear to everyone that the Virgin did not give birth to him. Some references to his earthly father and mother seem believable as well as what he says about his youth. However, the relationship between his father-in-law and his wife is less clear. His having three children is a fact. So, some of the facts P states are real, others are possible or probable. But a very large part of his perception of reality is *perceived* by Geelians as proof of his mental illness. These are not interpretations but apparent perceptible facts. One does not even have to judge what goes on in P's mind. He appears to the Geelians as someone who seriously 'flips,' a case in which there is not much one can do. We shall discuss the Geelians' definition of mental illness and mental patient later on. There is only slight similarity between P and a normal healthy being. He exists in a discontinuous pattern for the greater part of his behavior. His vision of his intimate identity, insofar he expresses it, is *different* and *less* than that of the healthy people. Interaction with him can only be felt as real insofar as the patient leaves behind his perspective of being God.

It is very unlikely that the host family and the Geel environment have driven P to consider himself as God's son by not accepting his viewpoint and his way of being, for example, because these did not correspond to their own 'bourgeois world' and order. Whatever the genesis or cause of P's deviation, he has always been 'God' and has never changed his attitude. He has not become God in Geel, and it is unlikely that a group of people can be found who are willing to take P seriously.

The Geelians who meet patients in bars or other public places all know cases very similar to those described above. With these examples in mind we shall now try to reconstruct the image of 'mental illness' and 'retardation' as it is viewed by the Geel endoculture. This image will be reconstructed from verbal expressions, verbalized attitudes, observed behavior, and the social structures of the home care system. We shall, in a word, attempt to outline the 'folk theory' of mental handicaps.

Then, we shall try to explain the existence of such a complex of images through a diachronic and contextual analysis. At the same time, we shall compare the Geel 'folk theory' to some scientific views on mental illness and retardation.

Geelian theory sees a break or a qualitative discontinuity between the 'normal' and the 'abnormal'. The 'people from the Kolonie,' the 'loonies', 'those from under the high trees,' and 'those that are in the book' (the register of the Rijkskolonie) are terms that specifically refer to the 'abnormals' in the system. The term 'boarder,' which has a more neutral sound and puts less emphasis on mental deficiency, is also used. The term 'patient' is rarely used. All the 'people from the Kolonie' have 'some reason to be in Geel,' something is wrong with all of them. Experience and the doctors have decided this, otherwise they would not be there. They 'flip' (lose contact with reality), are always 'above or below the line' (are not capable of keeping the right measure: They are either too cheerful or too passive), they are 'bossy' (are domineering, get themselves noticed, lose all sense of proportion in social relations), are bullheaded (are extremely stubborn or unmanageable), 'have fits' (of total unmanageability or aggressiveness their behavior often being unpredictable), or they are 'foolish,' 'childish,' 'don't make too much of it' (are at most only slightly involved in the surrounding reality, do not understand what is really happening). It is generally thought that they have these fits usually around the time of the major holidays: Christmas, New Year's, and Easter.

In all our research, we especially looked for a popular explanation of mental illness and mental feebleness. As a result, we may safely conclude that, on the level of crystallized thought of patterns (culture), there are no elaborated theories concerning mental deficiencies. All researchers on the team were struck by the fact that the Geelians involved never *spontaneously* tried to give an explanation about how this man or woman with whom they live became 'ill,' or what this 'illness' actually represents.

We can only mention one single spontaneous remark: "When X arrived here in Geel he was pitiful. Now they've driven him crazy." By this the informant meant to say that the way in which a pathetic man with a low IQ was treated was the direct cause of the fact that he now 'flips.' In all other cases explanations were offered only after we had explicitly asked the question. In most of the 70 in-depth interviews the answers were hesitant and short. "The patient's parents were drunks." "There's something wrong in the family." In other words, the 'illness' is explained through the effect of biological heredity in the popular sense of the word, or by the disastrous influence of social environment. These answers seem to be stereotypes.

Even with insistence we never came to any comprehensive explanation. This is not surprising because in most cases the host family does not know the patient's history or knows it only through vague indications. In many cases they have never met the patient's family, have never received information from outside sources, and can only refer to what the patient himself tells them. Many host families consider the boarder's stories to be unreliable. Hence, we may conclude that there is not much folk theory building in this field. In the course of the investigation it also became clear that no one sought any explanation in 'learned books.' Names like Freud, Kräpelin, Rümke, let alone Lacan and Eysenck, are totally unknown to them.

Although the deficiencies may or may not be biopsychological, the deviations the Geelians observe in their boarders are ascribed to *illness*. This is an illness more or less to be compared with other illnesses, but still a *mental illness*. This indicates that people feel something is wrong, somewhere within the patient, probably in his head, but they don't know what. Patients are cases for the 'doctor.' However, many patients are considered hopeless cases by the doctors as well. They will never recover. The district nurse brings drugs, 'pills' to many patients, the name of which none of the host families can recall. They only know that they usually help to 'calm them down.' Although we are not able to support this with statistics, we know for sure—as do all Geelians invol-ved—that many drugs are never taken by the patients. They are flushed down the toilet or put away by the family, usually because drugs often make things worse, or because the patient would disturb the host family's rhythm of life by sleeping in the daytime, during meals, or by incontinence, and so on. Many Geelians who have boarders are skeptical about the drugs. They think 'the right drugs' have not yet been invented for most cases. The doctors are not able to do much either. This skepticism with respect to chemical therapy may also be based on the fact that they have seen many patients recover without taking 'pills.'

No Geelian still believes that disturbances in the patient are caused by 'evil spirits' such as the devil. Such an opinion, which in former centuries may have been held and is con-tained in the St. Dympna legend, is now considered backward and ridiculous folklore. Mental illness is generally accepted as a medical problem.

Although a clear discontinuity or break between being healthy and being ill is perceived, a clear gradation in being ill is also recognized. There are good and bad boarders, and boarders in-between. There are, for example, patients who are good for a long period of time and then suddenly have 'fits,' generally around the time of the major holidays or when the leaves start falling. To outsiders interested in the patients at Geel, the Geelians stress that there are no boarders who are ill on all levels of life. They emphasize that the patients are not dangerous, that outsiders cannot distinguish many patients from the normal Geelians, that a lot of patients work very actively and efficiently together with the farmers and, as cheap laborers, help them to survive. Some patients ride bicycles, go to church services, soccer games, bars, and go for walks. And many boarders are very much 'with it,' in many different matters. In other words, the 'people from the Kolonie' are ill, not crazy. They are not people who are constantly deviant in all levels of life. The term 'crazy' is rarely if ever used and its employment in public establishments is felt to be rude and unacceptable. It usually provokes an immediate reaction from the public if it is used in a defamatory or disapproving manner.

According to the Geel endoculture, a boarder is never totally disturbed. He is always, in some way or other, socially or mentally normal. He always knows something, however little. He always has some feelings or other like those that move normal people. Mental illness or feebleness never comprises the entire person in all his aspects. For example, every Geelian knows Jules the Russian, an ex-patient who, as we mentioned before, was not only very capable in mathematics but, in an inexplainable way, exceptionally so. One regularly meets Geelians who tell you they were raised by patients, many of whom brought them to and from school. Also some patients were said to be more clever (had more schooling) than their host families and helped the children with their homework. Everyone in Geel knows that there used to be a band leader from the Kolonie[2]. There is a whole series of stories about patients who in one way or another functioned normally in daily life in Geel. Yet this does not detract from the fact that all patients are not 'right' at some point, and some patients at many.

The idea that the patients are never totally ill and the fact that they are given a chance to demonstrate their healthy aspects, even if the abnormal phenomena are never entirely absent, seem to us to be remarkable features of the Geel system, distinguishing it from all other average environments with average prejudices and perhaps from some mental hospitals. The host families find out by trial and error what the patients can manage, and from this determine certain limits.

We shall now try to explain the image of mental illness or feebleness that we observed as the common denominator in Geel, in the environments where patients regularly live by means of contextual and diachronic analysis.

First, we will explore the break between the normal and the pathological-abnormal. This Geel view can be explained by a series of factors.

A primary and very important factor seems to be the function of the Geel home care system as conceived by Belgian psychiatry. Psychiatrists, clinics, and hospitals send to Geel, almost exclusively, 'oligophrenics' and 'psychotics' who are not given much chance of recovery. Many of these people already have had a long career of treatment behind them in other medical institutions. Although among the Geel patients there are a few milder cases, the Rijkskolonie itself classifies its patients as oligophrenics and psychotics, i.e., 'exclusively serious cases.'

It is not superfluous to mention here that previously the patient population was composed predominantly of 'patients' sent to Geel for economic reasons by the welfare agencies of Brussels and other cities. Geel was much cheaper than a mental hospital. As we mentioned before Brussels closed its own institution in 1803 and had its patients transferred to Geel. As many other welfare agencies did the same, the number of patients increased from 200 in 1800 to 900 in 1850[3]. Patients from the more well-to-do families were not often sent to Geel, and this fact alone gave the town a bad reputation. Thus, Geelians belonging to environments that maintain face-to-face relationships with the patients primarily have contact with seriously deficient persons.

In former centuries and decades patients who had to be locked up regularly because they became dangerous and aggressive were also sent to Geel. We have often heard older Geelians refer to former times when 'tough guys' were still coming to Geel: The host fathers regularly had to fight them to keep them under control. That Geelians view deviant behavior as discontinuous with normal behavior cannot be called a prejudice. It is an opinion based on observable fact. Geelians seldom see 'mild cases' among the Rijkskolonie patients. Subsequently, they are not inclined to place patients on a continuum running from healthy to ill without a clear break. In Geel people who consider themselves normal and are recognized as such are daily confronted with other people who are seriously mentally ill. The result of this is that the opposition illness-health is seen as a black-white contrast. The ill are so ill that the healthy look eminently healthy.

So, the first factor explaining why the Geelians view the patients in a separate category seems to be that they are primarily confronted with serious cases—people who have, at least partially, designed for themselves a particular world view that is inaccessible to others and of limited value in terms of intersubjective relationships.

The second factor is that new people with these same characteristics are continually being brought in from the outside. This has been so for centuries and dates back prior to the affluent society, the airplane, the busy city life, capitalism, environmental pollution, and so on—at least since the thirteenth century. To the Geelians mental patients are by no means a phenomenon of our times. They are not specific products of 'modern hurried life.' There have been boarders for as long as one can look back into the past. The ancestors of the present Geelians have always been able to distinguish between normal and abnormal, and so have former societies. In the Geel situation mentally ill and retarded people appear as constant realities. They have always existed, they have always been different from others and, therefore, their existence as a separate category is beyond doubt.

The third reason why the 'people from the Kolonie' are viewed as different is the fact that they are recognized and named as such by professionals, doctors, and a state institution. They are 'in the book' (registered as patients).

Here, the problem of medical psychiatry emerges, and this provides another explanation for the division between normal and abnormal. It is clear that the official Geel system uses terms from the hospital world. People with mental problems are 'ill' or 'patients.' There is a 'hospital,' an 'infirmary.' The people in charge are physicians. There are nurses and district nurses. Drugs are given. There are regular medical checkups. Medical law concerning hospitals is applied. Patients are given 'care,' are being 'treated.' There are 'hospital' road signs to warn drivers. Patients 'recover' and are 'discharged.' In other words, medical and hospital jargon has been grafted onto the Geel system.

However, a number of terms that are different from hospital language have persisted. Geelians rarely or never speak about patients, but rather of 'boarders'—people who are taken in to board. Remarkably, it is the Rijkskolonie hospital, where the medical services are housed and the new patients are observed or unmanageable boarders are taken that fulfills the actual role of 'mental institution' not the Geel community. For example, a patient who is not compliant or threatens to become unmanageable will be told: "Look out or you go to Geel!" So with their host families, the boarders are not actually 'in Geel.' The hospital is a place a certain distance away, a place where one ends up when things turn out bad, a 'stick behind the door' for the host family. The district nurse is the representative of this institution. He can take boarders with him and put them in the ward if they are not compliant.

Host families are not nurses but simply host families. It is a well-known secret that many patients have not seen a doctor in years, and the district nurses do not appear primarily as medical or paramedical figures. Rather, as F. Cuvelier notes, they play the role of the maternal uncle in a matrilineal society, the man who represents the authority, the Rijkskolonie[4].

The fact that the majority of the patients do not live in a hospital removes the atmosphere of the hospital. The boarders are not numbers but 'Jeff' or 'Marie.' So far, the nosology of medical psychiatry has not found its way into the host families: schizophrenia, paranoia, manic-depressive psychosis, and so on, are terms which the Geelians involved have rarely, if ever, heard, and which they will certainly not remember. Of the drugs, they only know that some have a good effect, others none at all. In any case, many boarders do not receive any drugs.

So we may say that Geel has largely escaped medical psychiatry, and that it is still free to choose its orientation. Nevertheless, the fact remains that mental illness is always diagnosed by doctors, who also determine whether a patient is cured or not. It is the doctors who place people in the patient category or bar them from it. This status allotment is fully effective in Geel and contributes to determining whether someone is or is not considered as belonging to that special category of the 'people from the Kolonie.'

The Geel opinion does not differ from the hypotheses of many scientists: Many psychoanalysts acknowledge that there is a break between the seriously deficient and other people. Seriously deficient people lose contact with reality. Almost all analysts have long been convinced that these categories of deranged people did not qualify for psychoanalytical treatment. Freud himself was of this opinion, and many present-day analysts still hold this view[5]. Although basing themselves on other premises than psychoanalytic ones, behavior therapists are forced to acknowledge that they can do nothing for many a 'serious case.' Even though they insist it is still too early to construct explanatory theories, they must recognize that those who are called 'psychotics' in Geel—i.e., people who are not capable of functioning independently in daily life—cannot be equated with slightly deficient people and certainly not with normal people.

It is clear that neither psychoanalysis nor psychology have, as yet, been able to construct a general theory on mental derangement. However, one thing is certain: Both recognize at least two categories of behavior—normal and abnormal—no matter what terms are chosen. The one is not the other. If that were not the case therapists would not be needed. There is an endless discussion on the exact criteria used to distinguish normal from abnormal behavior and it is very probable that this discussion will never be closed because its sociocultural context is constantly changing. However, the fact that professionals cannot agree on a set of definitions and terms does not by any means imply that seriously deranged people could not be distinguished from normal people. For most cases—we are inclined to say for all cases—almost everyone would be able to identify the deranged as such. Many patients in Geel are even capable of qualifying the devaint behavior of other boarders as abnormal.

At any rate, the Geelians involved daily meet people whom they observe talking and acting in terms of a world or a symbolic system that only partly corresponds to their own. Boarders take fantasies for reality, see causal relationships where there cannot be such relationships, consider themselves to be someone else, tell rambling stories, make unreal evaluations of their relationships with other people and about their hallucinations so that Geelians cannot possibly follow them. Patient N's fears, when he has forgotten to take his 'pills' for a couple of days, that the Germans (from World War II) are after him—thus he should be hidden and protected—cannot be shared by the inhabitants of Geel. That patient P1, who takes himself for the second person of the Trinity, is not considered a basis for the revision of local or universal church teaching is no wonder either. Patient P2's assertion that at 80 she has been found pregnant by a doctor of the Rijkskolonie is not considered a fact with which the environment should reckon. And when another patient repeatedly claims to have lost half of his head and one of his hands while he is talking and everyone sees that everything is there, he is not considered reliable either. When everyone can observe an almost endless series of such facts, it seems absurd to view and judge the Geelians' opinions and behavior with respect to the patients in the light of ideological literature based primarily on the slogan, "A bas les différences!" One would rather be inclined to say: "We are all deranged."

In recent years voices have been raised in almost all countries of the Western world in favor of the 'oppressed minorities': the handicapped, divorced, homosexuals, pedophiliacs, prisoners, ex-prisoners, migrant workers, ethnic minorities, and so on. It is beyond doubt that abuses have been committed against these groups. There is oppression, exploitation, systematic neglect and no one will claim that these campaigns are useless. More specifically in the cases of handicapped persons, emphasis has been placed on the equality of these people with other people, for example, by introducing new terminology. The handicap remains, however, and is often observable to everyone. When we are dealing with seriously mentally handicapped persons, the handicapped are partially submerged in their deficiency, even as persons.

Thus, for example, in *Wie is van Hout* by Jan Foudraine, Carl Whitaker is quoted: "If a schizophrenic youngster comes in here and tells me what a horrible thing his mother and father did to him, I say, 'Look, you've got to give them credit. They made you crazy and you get something out of life. You're not out there dead like most of these characters carrying a briefcase.' I differentiate crazy from insane. The insane are what Christ called the 'whited sepulchers.' The ones who go to jobs every morning in gray flannel suits."

Interviewer: "A lot of people who work intensively with schizophrenics seem to get more of an appreciation of craziness and less of an appreciation of ordinary life."

Dr. W.: "It's true. I'm envious of people who have had an overt craziness. (I've had my moments and shades and shadows but never the full-blown creativity that some of these people have available to them.) They may never get around to using it, but they've got it right there."[6]

With these tendencies in mind the layman might think that people who are clearly different in one or many sectors of their behavior can be viewed and treated as if their world were just as real and as valuable as that of normal people. With respect to the Geel family care system, this implies that people should respond to the boarders' derangedness. This game, however, is untenable even for the best-trained therapist. Geelians are not confronted with one single deviant case but with dozens of deranged people. Every one of these boarders has constructed a particular piece of world and it would be impracticable to familiarize oneself thoroughly with each of these worlds. At a certain moment in a certain situation, the healthy Geelian must say: "Stop. I can't go any further, and I don't want to either!" No therapist thinks that the deviant reality of his client is just as good as his own, otherwise he would not be a therapist and certainly would not remain one. But in the *writings* of certain professionals this relativizing of normalcy may go so far that one has the impression that equality between the normal and the abnormal is not beyond possibility. Considering Geel home care from this perspective, the system could be judged unfavorable. The Geelians briefly go along with the patient's imaginary world by saying: "You're right" or by keeping silent, but they never take this game seriously. They clearly start from the view that the patients, through their deviations, are not only *different* but also *less* than themselves. This being *less* appears to be self-evident. And there is a specific reason for this obviousness: The particular subsystem developed by patients concerning reality never becomes viable, accessible to others, or a basis on which something can be constructed. That is why their deviant behavior is not only different but also of less or no value. As Whitaker says in the above-mentioned quotation: They are unable to *use* their creativity. Their world, insofar as it is imaginary, is not accessible to intersubjective communication in which others can take part. Perhaps certain therapists feel at ease in such a situation and may even acquire a desire to be in their patient's condition, but Geelians have never felt this way.

Geelians can hardly be expected to see the imaginary world of their boarders as a meaningful alternative system, something comparable to another people's culture. So far it has always seemed that every ethnic group has its own 'mentally ill' or 'deviant' people. Every culture distinguishes between the living and the dead, these people are also connot mean to be just anything. And although some people who, in our society, would be classified as patients could perhaps in other cultures assume influential positions as fortune-tellers, as being possessed by spirits, or as mediators between the living and the dead; these people are also considered by their environment as belonging to the abnormal sphere. Moreover, it would be a serious mistake to maintain that all mental deviants are seen as a kind of chosen people.

When the Geelians recognize the boarders' deviations as such and react to them as we have described in the preceding chapters, they do exactly as is done all over the world, but perhaps more dexterously. There is nothing of misplaced discrimination in Geel nor of a very special approach.

Furthermore, the question remains as to whether the joking relationship with patients has negative effects on the latters' mental state. To answer this question is not within our competence, but it deserves the full attention of psychologists and psychiatrists because it touches on the very core of the Geel system. This question can also be formulated in a different way: Do the Geelians, by their differential attitude towards the patients, keep them ill? As anthropologists we can only state an opinion based on anthropological literature. It has been observed, for example, that in certain ethnic groups, severe depression, characterized by apathy, inactivity, and the like, is not felt to be or treated as an abnormal state[7]. People in such a state are not considered to be disturbed or mentally ill. However, this does not imply that their condition ceases to exist or improves in a spectacular manner, which shows that language is not omnipotent[8]. Mental disturbances need not have a name in order to exist.

And one may wonder whether the social marking of a deviant characteristic indeed confirms this characteristic when we are dealing with a marking of the soft type as we have described above. To this the question may be added whether the considerable attention paid to deviations would not augment these deviations, which in the end would render the cohabitation of boarders and Geelians impossible.

We don't see how the Geel public, in the streets, in public places, could behave differently from the way it behaves now, and we seriously wonder if every intervention attempting to change these interaction patterns—assuming this were possible—would not endanger an acquisition of centuries of experience and tradition.

Although we confined our research in Geel strictly within the compass of social and cultural anthropology and avoided the formulation of 'more comprehensive' statements, we still have had to grapple continuously with the question of the psychological and therapeutical value of the Geel system.

We are of the opinion that it is *technically* impossible to determine the degree to which each of the interactions in which the patients are involved *outside of the host family* promote or detract from their mental health. With the present state of our knowledge the only thing one can do is to presume that the influence brought to bear on the patient *outside* the host family is comparable to that exercised *within* the host family. And what happens within the host family is easier to observe and study.

On the therapeutic value of the interaction within the host family, there is a scientific study available by Dr. F. Cuvelier, *La famille nourricière de Gheel comme micro-communauté thérapeutique* (*The Host Family of Geel as a Therapeutic Micro-Community*)[9]. As we have already mentioned, Dr. Cuvelier's work was part of the Geel Project. He carried out his research during the period from October 1 1967 to September 30 1971, living in Geel in that time. His work is complementary to ours as he focused his attention on the interactions occurring *within* the host families and studied them not from an anthropological but from a sociopsychological point of view.

In planning his work Dr. Cuvelier assumed that the first two years of residence in a host family were probably the most important for the further development of the relations between the boarder and the host family. Therefore, he observed the development of the interaction patterns of 32 new patients and their host families over a period of two years. These 32 patients were chosen such that there were 16 men and 16 women, and 16 'schizophrenics' and 16 'oligophrenics.' There were 16 families who had had experience with boarders, and 16 for whom this was the first time.

Dr. Cuvelier regularly visited each of these families at various times of the day and carried out direct observations for periods from 35 to 65 minutes. He recorded 5,100 'alteractions,' a term which he defines as "an interpersonal action by which one person does something in relation to another person (from the Latin *alter* meaning 'other' and *actus* meaning 'action'). . . . The syntax of these *alteractions* or their mutual consonance forms the base of the more complex structure of interaction."[10] Using a system he developed following Lévi-Strauss, Schutz, Longabaugh, and others,[11] he classified these 5,100 alteractions. After processing this material quantitatively, Dr. Cuvelier arrived at a conclusion that we may summarize as follows: In the great majority of the host families there is a clear 'mental promotion' of the patient or boarder, and this improvement is primarily on the psychosocial level. The boarder learns to employ a more diversified range of alteractions to an increasing degree. In this sense the boarders 'develop' themselves.

During the first three months the boarders are subservient and docile and keep aloof. After this they pass through a period of negativistic reaction that lasts to the sixth month: The patient rejects any direction, help, or information given by the members of the host family. A turning point occurs during the second half of the first year: The boarder begins to be helpful, becomes more open to contact, and starts to express feelings of appreciation. They become more autonomous. The eighteenth to the twenty-fourth month is a period of stabilization: The behavior of the boarder continues to be marked by willingness to help, receptivity, and openness. The tendency to opposition virtually disappears. During the first year the patient does things that belong to the 'role of the sick person,' particularly in the initial, passive phase. In the course of the second year more and more actions appear that one associates with a 'normal role.' We can state, therefore, that the boarder learns 'normal behavior' in the host family, and unlearns 'deviant behavior'[12].

Dr. Cuvelier summarizes the way in which this occurs as follows: The Geel host family can be characterized as a 'matrifamily.' "The host family thus forms a small institution with three bearers of stable functions: the husband, who plays the affective role and who is the 'closest,' could be considered equivalent to an accepting Rogerian therapist; the wife could be considered equivalent to a structural and behavioral therapist; and the nurse takes on the function of the sanctioning authority. The division of the socioaffective function into two different male figures permits, perhaps, the boarders to clarify better their own reactions to the various aspects of the father figure."[13]

Nevertheless, according to Dr. Cuvelier, the importance of the structuring component must not be exaggerated. Even though many directives are given to the patient—28% of the alteractions are of this nature--the 'treatment' in the family context is still characterized by the absence of restraint. By way of comparison with the average American family, 36% of the total alteractions (from the parents to the children) are directive[14].

The process of fitting into the family does not proceed in the same manner for the 'schizophrenics' as for the 'oligophrenics.' 'Schizophrenics' avoid contact with their surroundings much more than do 'oligophrenics.' Still, the number of contacts intiated by the 'schizophrenics' is much higher than their attempts to avoid contact: Cuvelier counted 250 as opposed to 120[15] .

Thus, it seems that the Geel system also exercises a certain beneficial effect on 'schizophrenics.'

By way of an overall evaluation of the family care system, Dr. Cuvelier states: "A definitive answer to the question of the curative value of the host families cannot yet be given. It opens wide possibilities that depend on the motivation and the relational aptitude of the host families."[16]

"Some of these families could be capable of reception with a therapeutic effect. . . . With others, a placement could be a therapeutic catastrophy if there is no attention given to, or interest in, the patient, or if the family does not try to integrate him. . . . For many the results fall between the two extremes. Generally, the host families are situated on the good side of the range. This tendency is reinforced by a natural selection process: Boarders do not stay as readily in host families that are therapeutically deficient. But these 'trials and errors' are not always without consequences."[17]

"The 'treatment by members of the family' seems to be characterized by the following: Above all, there is a reciprocal belief in interpersonal accommodation and the necessity for flexibility. This belief must be held by the family as well as by the boarder. We consider this flexibility in the context with the other as the motor of the sociotherapeutic action of family care at Geel.[18] "

It can reasonably be presumed that the broader milieu of the Geel community affects the patients according to modalities that are analogous to those encountered *within* the host family. Some 'alteractions' with 'normal' Geelians will indeed have deleterious effects on some patients, while others will be beneficial. But further than this *hypothesis* we cannot go. And with this we do not yet know *the degree* to which this form of therapy, on the mental level, is more efficient than the forms of therapy found in the average institution.

As far as numbers are concerned, Geel does not 'discharge'

very many patients. The table below gives some idea of the range of these numbers:

Patient Discharges (and Losses)[19,20]			
Reason	*1976*	*1975*	*1974*
Discharges after improvement	36	29	30
Discharges after trial leave	3	7	5
Transfers to other institutions (patient unsuitable for family care)	14	14	7
Returns to institutions of origin (patient unsuitable for family care)	8	16	12
Death:			
Sickness	58	54	56
Accident	3	–	–
Suicide	2	–	–
Escape: Departure on own initiative	–	1	–

It must be kept in mind when interpreting these figures that Geel receives predominantly 'oligophrenics' and 'chronic cases' that already have a long institutional history.

Though the curative efficiency of the Geel system is difficult to express in numbers, we are certain of one thing: Practically *all* the patients like it better there than in the institution or institutions from where they came. The greatest threat hanging over them is another period of confinement 'inside.' This piece of 'subjective' data, which is irrefutable, indicates that Geel is a human milieu not only in the eyes of the observer-anthropologist, but also for the boarders, even though 'one is not cured quickly there.' Many of the boarders were not cured in 'institutions' either, and certainly not quickly. Otherwise they would not be in Geel.

NOTES

1. See, for example, J. Foudraine, *Wie is van Hout. Een Gang door de Psychiatrie*, Bilthoven, Amboboeken, 1971, passim. Also, K. Trimbos, *Anti-*

psychiatrie. Een Overzicht. Deventer, Van Loghum Slaterus, 1975.

2. Ignace Colbert (1751-1843), see W. Van Broeckhoven, Cultuur en Kunst in het Verleden. In *Geel*, p. 148.

3. K. Veraghtert, unpublished report.

4. F. Cuvelier, *De Interaktie tussen Psychiatrisch Patiënt en Geels Pleeggezin*.

5. See W. Hubert, H. T. Piron, and A. Vergote, *Psycho-Analyse. Wetenschap van de Mens*. Antwerp, De Nederlandsche Boekhandel, 1966, p. 96. Also, A. Vergote's oral communications.

6. Foudraine, op. cit., pp. 450-451. After checking this citation in the original English version, we noticed that Foudraine took these words slightly out of context, thus making them sound more radical than Whitaker perhaps intended. But the fact that Foudraine cited Whitaker in this way clearly reflects what Foudraine himself has in mind and what he sees in it. The parentheses portion of the passage was not cited by Foudraine. The original text is from J. Haley and L. Hoffman, *Techniques of Family Therapy*. New York–London, Basic Books, 1967, p. 282.

7. J. Kennedy, Cultural Psychiatry, p. 1,141.

8. Authors such as Foudraine uncritically adopt positions like the Sapir-Whorf hypothesis. For a more critical approach, see J. Tennekes, *Anthropology, Relativism and Method. An Inquiry into the Methodological Principles of a Science of Culture*, Assen, Van Gorcum, 1971.

9. Article published in *L'information psychiatrique*, Vol. 52, no. 8, October 1976, pp. 915-930.

10. Ibidem, p. 916.

11. Ibidem, p. 917.

12. Ibidem, p. 929.

13. Ibidem, pp. 922-923.

14. Ibidem, p. 923.

15. Ibidem.

16. Ibidem, p. 929.

17. Ibidem.

18. Ibidem, p. 930.

19. See J. Segers, *Sociologische Doorlichting van het R.P.Z.-C.V.G.*, p. 9.

20. On January 1 1978 there were still 1,340 patients in Geel, 1,082 were residing in families and the rest in the central hospital[21]. The patient population has significantly decreased over the last few years: There are now 250 patients less than at the time of our study.

21. See Dr. J. Wouters, *Voorlopig Verslag over het Holvenprojekt*, unpublished report, 1978, p. 1. We thank this author for giving us permission to use his report in the preparation of this book and for providing us with the reports of Dr. H. Matheussen and J. Segers.

Chapter 11

CONCLUSIONS CONCERNING

THEORY AND POLICY

(1) Hundreds of years of coexistence of normal people and mental patients did not result in a subculture where the line between the normal and the abnormal-pathological is erased. Although many Geelians grew up in families where patients were often present, they do not perceive or experience the boarders' deviant behavior as an extreme form of 'alternative' personal culture. They feel that there is definitely something wrong with such behavior. Abnormalcy is for everyone clearly pathological, ill, or morbid. So the popular saying which we quoted in the beginning is not valid: All of Geel is *not* half crazy. However hard to define, an intuitive feeling of what is normal and what is abnormal seems to be within the capacities of normal human beings and even of many deranged people when it pertains to deviant behavior of other patients.

(2) Normalcy in contacts with patients is constantly maintained through a subtle play of joking relations. Only in cases

of need are patients reprimanded or is the psychiatric hospital called in. Thus, the healthy population continues to express and apply its standards of normalcy in many varying situations, in this way keeping itself at a safe distance from delusion.

(3) This normalcy is constantly shown to the patients in all sectors of social life that are accessible to them as a possibility and as an invitation. By trial and error in daily life, it is determined how far the patient can be allowed to venture autonomously into the local community. This situation is clearly different from the one found in institutions, where the environment consists of people who have somehow lost normalcy. In an institution, daily, normal life is almost totally lacking, and the hospital staff who set the standards, operate necessarily within the framework of a 'hospital situation.'

(4) Many patients do not seem repelled by the normalcy shown them by the Geelians in all kinds of situations. As demonstrated in the previous chapters, many boarders are fond of meeting people or watching them work outside the host family environment. Patients do not tend to form closed groups or associate only with those groups.

(5) In many 'chronic' cases it is not sufficient to take mentally deranged persons from their original environment and put them in another normal environment to bring about their recovery. The fact that countless patients have spent their entire lives in Geel is clear proof of this. A favorable social environment does not solve everything.

(6) An average, medium-sized community is easily capable of adopting hundreds of mentally deranged or feeble-minded persons who have been taken out of their original environment without suffering significant negative effects on its social life. Such an operation does not involve insurmountable sociotechnical problems. Everything depends on what the community involved wants. If it demands that its environment be as 'hygienic' and 'esthetic' as possible so as to be

able to enjoy its prosperity in an ideal (utopian) fashion, it should not adopt such patients. Modern prosperity, the effects of which are felt in Geel, opposes the Geel system: The public of the discotheques and of the establishments for the wealthier and more educated people, as well as those families 'that don't need it,' prefer to keep aloof from the boarders. This raises the question of who is more *ethically* advanced: the traditional host family that keeps its boarder because he provides some income and because he has become part of the family, or the 'modern people' who frown on boarders. It seems that technological, economic, and cultural 'development' does not make the entire system better *for everyone.*

(7) The irrefutable fact that internment in the psychiatric hospital is felt by all patients as a severe punishment shows, apart from all subtle measurements, that boarders much prefer to stay with their host family and in the Geel community than in an institution, even if the latter provides a very human environment, good food, and optimal care. The patients' many different disturbances and handicaps apparently do not prevent them from being unanimously convinced that an institution is still an institution.

(8) The previous chapters have shown that the Geelians who regularly deal with patients are not afraid of mentally deranged persons, that they learn to distinguish whatever positive dimensions are present in the patient, and that they give the apparently healthy aspects of the patient a chance. Patients who are capable of walking, working, going to bars, and so on, are allowed to do so. Therefore, actual, direct contacts favor the patients' social integration. Newcomers in Geel who adopted patients all state that they went through an adjustment period in which they were suspicious and somewhat afraid in the presence of the patients, but that their mistrust gradually disappeared.

To bring normals in direct contact with mental patients in a 'natural' environment seems to be the best, and probably the only efficient means of eliminating prejudices and promoting the integration of the patients. To put it bluntly: Most people tend to see many 'crazy people' as crazier than they are, and by direct contact this tendency is corrected in favor of the mental patients.

This conclusion seems very important in the light of further action. In setting up a project aimed at duplicating the Geel system, we do not think it advisable to spend much time on 'mental reconversion' of the families by information and discussion in the conceptual and verbal fields. It is perhaps preferable to devote more time to mapping out the social network so as to locate the key figures in the local community. These key figures need not be the local authorities, but rather persons who, by their many contacts with other members of the community, perform an interfacing role. If one succeeds in lodging a few patients with such key figures, by way of probation, chances are high that a large portion of the community will soon be convinced that life with mental patients is not as terrible as generally believed. In other words, we may speculate on the fact that actual contact with deranged persons *outside the environment where the derangement originated* will act in favor of the deranged persons and that their image will benefit from their confrontation with normal people. This is an important lesson that can be drawn from the Geel experiment.

This also implies that negative prejudices against mental patients are considerably augmented if these people are removed from normal social intercourse. This does not mean, however, that it will not be necessary to advise these people to leave their original environment which for them was a source of conflict.

It seems specific for Geel that nearly all people with whom the patients come into contact have become convinced of the fact that living with mental patients is possible, not dangerous, not contagious, and altogether less difficult than 'naive,' inexperienced outsiders think.

As one Geelian, a psychiatrist at the Rijkskolonie, said in a speech: "Geel is special in that it is such an ordinary town."

In Geel, people succeed in living with seriously handicapped persons in a manner that is acceptable to most of those involved. Geel has been doing it for centuries.

Therefore, it would be paradoxical that the Geel system would disappear now in a time when integration of deranged or handicapped persons in normal society is being seriously proposed and when almost everyone considers institutions as a temporary solution acceptable only for the most serious cases.

Nevertheless, the Geel system is threatened.

Generally speaking, the allowances paid by the State to the host families are no real compensation for the care given to the patients. Young people find more rewarding forms of work that also better correspond with the perspectives of a young family intending to live in a more urban fashion. Should the authorities not change their policy, there is a danger that host families will be selected in an ever more negative way: only people will be available who cannot find employment in other sectors. Big farmers who have introduced mechanization no longer have much need for help from unskilled patients, and small farmers for whom unskilled labor might still be helpful now risk losing their farms and they will not be replaced. It is completely unrealistic to expect from the Geel population a sort of idealistic selflessness or charity and to hope that they will continue patient care almost gratuitously. This type of idealism cannot be found in Geel and probably never existed. After everything we have written in this book, it should be clear that this observation is not one of disapproval. We only want to stress that the system will be ruined when one does not recognize its economic reality. Policy makers cannot ignore the fact that Geel is a remarkable achievement. Not only in the host families but in the overall community as well, there is a tradition of dealing with mental patients that would require an immense mental and social effort to reproduce elsewhere. Bearing in mind how other groups behave towards mental patients, one becomes aware of what the Geel community, as a community, has accomplished.[1]

The sociocultural and economic development of Geel and its effect on family care may be represented as a solid reality whose 'harmful' effects are unavoidable. But we may also attempt to neutralize these effects. Everything depends on what we want.

It is indeed not improbable that the Geel system may be continued by paying allowances that make boarding attractive to housewives. We think that it is sufficient to hold out the prospect of this adaptation of allowances and gradually but sensibly to implement it in order to obtain the desired effect.

Moreover, the therapeutic achievements of psychiatry and clinical psychology may be put to the service of the limited number of boarders who are capable of recovery, so that these patients in Geel are given the same opportunities as those housed in institutions or in open homes. In terms of the national social care budget, this could be realized with a very small amount of money. Experts with long experience in Geel are willing to cooperate in a cautious trial of the necessary adjustments. It is very probable that they will succeed, in view of the understanding and favorable conditions present in the Geel environment.

Whoever writes off Geel does this by his own judgment, not because the system's disappearance is inevitable nor because maintenance of the Geel system would cost the Belgian community excessive amounts.

The Geelians would not be the greatest victims of a negative decision. These would be the many handicapped persons who for the rest of their lives would be unable to function adequately in a normal environment elsewhere.

Although it is probable that the boarders will always remain a special type of people, in Geel they are accepted as

such, for their bad as well as primarily, for their good sides.
For them, life is human 'under the high trees.'

NOTES

1. See J. RABKIN, Public Attitudes Towards Mental Illness: A Review of the
Literature. *Schizophrenia Bulletin* 10 (1974), pp. 9-33. See also: A. ASKENASY,
Attitudes Toward Mental Patients. A study Across Cultures, The Hague, Mouton,
1974.

The last of 'the tall trees' along one of the roads that pass by the State Psychiatric Hospital.

REFERENCES

ASKENASY, A., *Attitudes Toward Mental Patients. A Study Across Cultures,* The Hague, Mouton, 1974.

BINSWANGER, H., Die Familienpflege im Kanton Zürich 1909-1936. Medizinische Erfahrungen. *Monatschrift für Psychiatrie und Neurologie,* Beiheft 87 (1939), pp. 1-128.

BOUWEN, R., *Sociaal-Psychologische Studiegroep,* Leuven, unpublished report, The Geel Family Care Research Project.

CHANTRAINE, J., Evolution actuelle du placement familial psychiatrique des adultes à Lierneux. *Acta Neurologica et Psychiatrica Belgica,* 68 (1968), 6, pp. 392-406.

CONSCIENCE, H., *Eene Gekkenwereld,* Antwerp, J.P. Van Dieren, 1881.

CUVELIER, F., *De Interaktie tussen Psychiatrisch Patiënt en Geels Pleeggezin,* Leuven, Faculty of Psychology and Education, doctoral thesis, 1974.

– – – Een Gastgezin als Kleine Therapeutiche Gemeenschap. *Tijdschrift voor Psychotherapie,* 1, (1975) 2, pp. 71-79.

DE BONT, M., De H. Dimpna. In *Geel. Van Gisteren tot Morgen,* Geel, Lions Mol-Geel, 1976, pp. 467-476.

DE SMET, W., Sociaal-Cultureel Verenigingsleven. In *Geel. Van Gisteren tot Morgen,* Geel, Lions Mol-Geel, 1976, pp. 399-401.

D'HERTEFELT-BRUYNOOGHE, R.-M., *Gezinsverplegingspatronen te Geel. Een Sociologisch Onderzoek vanuit Kostgezinnen en Patiënten,* Leuven, Leuven University Press, 1975.

DUMONT, M. P. and C. K. ALDRICK, Family Care after a Thousand Years. A Crisis in the Tradition of St. Dympna. *American Journal of Psychiatry,* 119 (1962) 2, pp. 116-121.

DUPRE, J., Economische Ontwikkeling en Industrializatie. In *Geel. Van Gisteren tot Morgen,* Geel, Lions Mol-Geel, 1976, pp. 288-307.

EYNIKEL, H., *De Uitbreiding en de Beoordeling van de Gezinsverpleging van Geesteszieken. Uitstraling van het Schotse en Geelse Systeem (1850-1970),* Leuven, Faculty of Philosophy and Letters, M.A. thesis, 1971.

– – – Geel, Bakermat van de Gezinsverpleging. *Annalen van de Belgische Vereniging voor Hospitaalgeschiedenis,* 9, 1971, pp. 113-123.

FOUDRAINE, J., *Wie is van Hout. Een Gang door de Psychiatrie,* Bilthoven, Amboboeken, 1971.

GOMINET, P., *Contribution à l'étude de l'assistance des malades mentaux en placement familial*, Paris, Faculty of Medicine, thesis, 1962.

GREENLAND, C., Family Care of Mental Patients. *American Journal of Psychiatry*, 119 (1963) 10, p. 1000.

HEDEBOUW, G., *Houding ten aanzien van Geel en de Geelse Gezinsverpleging. Overzicht van Onderzoeksresultaten van het Sociaal-Psychologisch Team van het Geel Family Care Research Project*, Leuven, unpublished report, 1975.

HONIGMANN, J. J., Sampling in Ethnographic Field Work. In R. Naroll and R. Cohen (Eds.), *A Handbook of Method in Cultural Anthropology*, New York, Columbia University Press, 1973, pp. 267-274.

HUBER, W., H. T. PIRON and A. VERGOTE, *Psycho-Analyse. Wetenschap van de Mens*. Antwerp, De Nederlandsche Boekhandel, 1966.

KENNEDY, J., Cultural Psychiatry. In J.J. Honigmann (Ed.), *Handbook of Social and Cultural Anthropology*, Chicago, Rand McNally, 1973, p. 1,183.

KOYEN, M. H., Gezinsverpleging van Geesteszieken te Geel tot Einde 18de Eeuw. *Jaarboek van de Vrijheid en Het Land van Geel*, 12, 1973.

KOYEN, M. H. and M. DE BONT, *Geel doorheen de Eeuwen Heen*. Geel, 1975.

KUYPERS, F. and K. VERAGHTERT, Het Geels Rijkspsychiatrisch Ziekenhuis: Een Micro-Economische Cel als Regionale Welvaartsfactor. In *Geel. Van Gisteren tot Morgen*, Geel, Lions Mol-Geel, 1976, pp. 447-491.

PALS-GHOOS, A., *Sociologisch Onderzoek naar de Gevolgen van Industrialisering in een Rekonversiegebied*, Leuven, Sociological Research Institute, Catholic University of Leuven, 1972, Rapport 1972/1973.

––– Maatschappelijke Verschijnselen tijdens Industriële Expansie. In *Geel. Van Gisteren tot Morgen*, Geel, Lions Mol-Geel, 1976, pp. 311-314.

––– Structuur van de Gemeente Geel. In *Geel. Van Gisteren tot Morgen*, Geel, Lions Mol-Geel, 1976, pp. 315-329.

––– Demografie. In *Geel. Van Gisteren tot Morgen*. Geel, Lions Mol-Geel, 1976, pp. 345-364.

RABKIN, J., Public Attitudes Toward Mental Illness: A Review of the Literature. *Schizophrenia Bulletin*, 10 (1974), pp. 9-33.

RADCLIFFE-BROWN, A. R., *Structure and Function in Primitive Society*, London, Cohen and West, 1963.

SROLE, L., *The Geel Family Care Project: Introduction*, Geel, Internationaal Symposium over Gezinsverpleging voor Geesteszieken, 1975, unpublished paper.

TENNEKENS, J., *Anthropology, Relativism and Method: An Inquiry into the Methodological Principles of a Science of Culture*, Assen, Van Gorcum, 1971.

TRIMBOS, K., *Antipsychiatrie. Een Overzicht*, Deventer, Van Loghum Slaterus, 1975.

VAN BROECKHOVEN, W., Cultuur en Kunst in het Verleden. In *Geel. Van Gisteren tot Morgen*, Geel, Lions Mol-Geel, 1976, pp. 89-178.

VERAGHTERT, K., De Overheid en de Geelse Gezinsverpleging (1660-1860). *Annalen van de Belgische Vereniging voor Hospitaalgeschiedenis*, 1969, VII, pp. 113-127.

––– De Geelse Gezinsverpleging als Regionale Welvaartsfactor (1795-1860). *Bijdragen tot de Geschiedenis*, 1971, pp. 3-30.

––– De Krankzinnigenverpleging te Geel (1795-1860). *Jaarboek van de Vrijheid en Het Land van Geel,* 1972, 11, pp. 1-148.

––– Unpublished contribution to 'International Symposium over Gezinsverpleging voor Geesteszieken', Geel, May 15 and 16, 1975.

––– Geel: Nationaal en Internationaal Verplegingsoord. In *Geel. Van Gisteren tot Morgen.* Geel, Lions Mol-Geel, 1976, pp. 492-507.

WHITING, B. and J. WHITING, Methods for Observing and Recording Behavior. In R. Naroll and R. Cohen (Eds.), *A Handbook of Method in Cultural Anthropology,* New York, Columbia University Press, 1973, pp. 282-286.

ABOUT THE AUTHOR

EUGEEN ROOSENS is Professor at the Katholieke Universiteit Leuven, Chairman of the Interfaculty Institute for Family and Sexological Sciences, and Director of the Postgraduate Formation and Research Program in Social and Cultural Anthropology. Since 1960 he has been conducting regular studies on the social relations between groups in greatly differing cultures (acculturation): 1960-1965 in Central Africa (about the Yaka), 1968-1969 with Indians in Northern Canada, and since 1974 he has been leading a team (sponsored by the Ford Foundation) studying ethnic relations in Morocco, Sicily, Belgium, and Bolivia.